Revision  s

Higher

Chemistry

D A Buchanan

(Moray House Institute,
Edinburgh University)

J R Melrose

(Lenzie Academy,
Lenzie, Glasgow)

assisted by J M Briggs

Stevenson College Library
Bankhead Avenue
EDINBURGH EH11 4DE

Published by
Chemcord
Inch Keith
East Kilbride
Glasgow

ISBN   1 870570 66 9

© Buchanan and Melrose, 1999

Reprint 2001
Reprint 2005

Typeset by J M Briggs
Printed by Bell and Bain Ltd, Glasgow

Contents

Unit 1 - Energy Matters

1.1   Following the course of a reaction
1.2   Factors affecting rate
1.3   Mole calculations
1.4   Calculations based on equations
1.5   The idea of excess
1.6   Catalysts
1.7   Potential energy diagrams
1.8   Enthalpy changes
1.9   Atomic and ionic size
1.10 Ionisation energy and
      electronegativity
1.11 Types of bonding and structure
1.12 Intermolecular forces of attraction
1.13 Polarity of molecules
1.14 Bonding and structure - the elements
1.15 Properties of substances
X 1.16 The Avogadro constant
1.17 Molar volumes of gases
1.18 Calculations involving volumes

Unit 2 - The World of Carbon

2.1   Fuels
2.2   Nomenclature and structural formulae
      - hydrocarbons
2.3   Nomenclature and structural formulae
      - alkanols
2.4   Nomenclature and structural formulae
      - alkanals, alkanones and alkanoic acids
2.5   Nomenclature and structural formulae
      - esters
2.6   Nomenclature and structural formulae
      - aromatic compounds
2.7   Cracking
2.8   Addition reactions
2.9   Primary, secondary and tertiary alcohols
2.10 Oxidation
2.11 Making and breaking esters
2.12 Percentage yields
2.13 Uses of carbon compounds
2.14 Early plastics and fibres (i)
2.15 Early plastics and fibres (ii)
2.16 Recent developments
2.17 Fats and oils
2.18 Proteins
2.19 Miscellaneous

Unit 3 - Chemical Reactions

3.1   The chemical industry
3.2   Hess's law
3.3   Equilibrium
3.4   The pH scale
3.5   Strong and weak acids and bases
3.6   The pH of salt solutions
3.7   Oxidising and reducing agents
3.8   Redox titratons
3.9   Electrolysis
3.10 Radioactivity
3.11 Nuclear equations
3.12 Artificial radioisotopes
3.13 Half-life

Prescribed Practical Activities

Problem Solving

Note to teachers and lecturers

The exercises are specifically written to test students' understanding of the key ideas in the Higher Chemistry (Higher Still) course and to give students practice in the kinds of questions used in the examination. They have been trialled over a number of years and found to be an invaluable revision aid.

The exercises are, by and large, independent of each other and consequently they can be used to fit almost any teaching order. They can be used in a variety of situations, e.g. self-study time in school, homework.

The variation in the length of the exercises is a reflection of the different types of questions which are associated with a particular part of the course. Teachers / lecturers may wish to focus on areas which are known to be difficult for their students.

A book of answers to the revision questions is also available.

Acknowledgement

A number of the questions in the exercises come from or have evolved from questions used in the SCE examinations. The publisher wishes to thank the Scottish Qualifications Authority for permission to use examination questions in these ways.

Unit 1   Energy Matters

Exercise 1.1   Following the course of a reaction

1. In the reaction **R → P**, the concentration of the reactants was measured at
    regular time intervals.
    a) Draw a rough graph to show how the concentration of reactants
        (y-axis) changes with time. (Label it **R**.)
    b) Add a curve to show the change in concentration of the products
        with time. (Label it **P**.)
    c) How do the gradients of the curves relate to the reaction speed?

2. Consider the following graph.

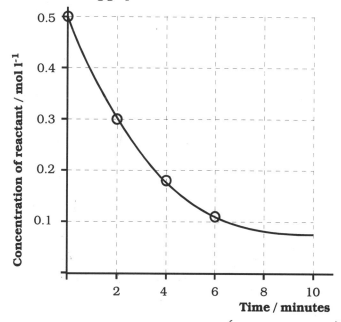

a) Calculate the average rate of reaction over the periods
    i) 0 to 2 minutes,   ii) 2 to 4 minutes,   iii) 4 to 6 minutes.
b) i) What happens to the reaction rate as the reaction proceeds?
    ii) Explain your answer.

3.   The following graph shows how the volume of the hydrogen produced in a
     reaction of excess magnesium with dilute acid varies with time.

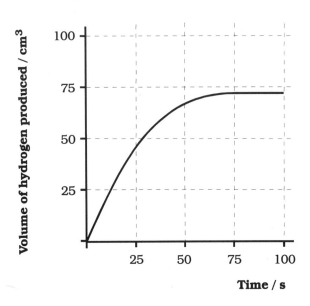

a)   What is the total volume of hydrogen produced in the reaction?
b)   i) How long does it take for the reaction to go to completion?
     ii) How long does it take for half of the hydrogen ions in the acid to
         be reduced to hydrogen?
     iii) Explain why your answer to ii) is not half your answer to i).
c)   Calculate the average rate of reaction over the first 25 s.

4.   The reaction between magnesium and dilute hydrochloric acid

                 Mg(s)   +   2HCl(aq)   →   MgCl$_2$(aq)   +   H$_2$(g)

     is followed on a top pan balance.

a)   Why do the balance readings show a decrease in mass as the reaction
     proceeds?
b)   Draw a rough graph to show how the balance readings (y-axis) vary
     with time for the reaction.

5. The overall rate of a reaction is often taken as the reciprocal of time (1/time). A graph of rate of reaction against temperature is shown below.

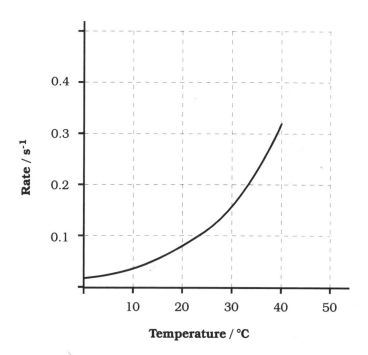

Temperature / °C

a) Calculate the time for the reaction when the temperature is 20 °C.
b) Find the temperature rise required to double the rate of the reaction.
c) Calculate the rate of the reaction at 50 °C.
d) Calculate the time taken for the reaction at
    i) 10°C,   ii) 20°C,   iii) 30°C.

6. a) Draw a rough graph to show how the volume of gas produced (y-axis) varies with time for the reaction:

    $$CaCO_3(s) \ + \ 2HCl(aq) \ \rightarrow \ CaCl_2(aq) \ + \ CO_2(g) \ + \ H_2O(l)$$

    b) For the same reaction, draw a second graph to show how the reaction rate varies with time.

7. Part of a chemistry project involved the study of the reaction between methyl ethanoate and sodium hydroxide solution.

$$CH_3COOCH_3(aq) + OH^-(aq) \rightarrow CH_3COO^-(aq) + CH_3OH(aq)$$

The graph below shows the results for one of the experiments.

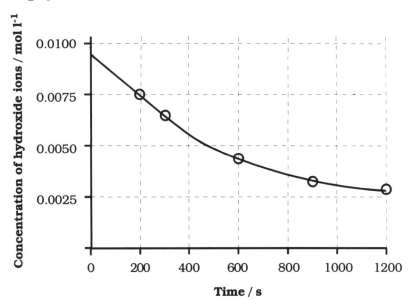

a) What was the initial concentration of the sodium hydroxide solution?

b) Calculate the average rate of reaction between 200 and 400 s.

c) Explain why this was different from the average rate of the reaction during the first 200 s of the reaction.

8. Marble chips, calcium carbonate, reacted with excess dilute hydrochloric acid. The rate of reaction was followed by recording the mass of the container and the reaction mixture over a period of time.
    The results of an experiment are shown in the following graph.

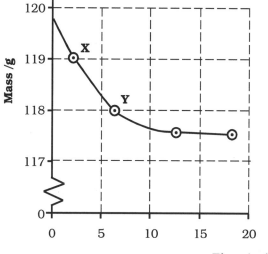

a) How does the rate of reaction at **X** compare with that at **Y**?
b) Calculate the average rate of reation over the first 5 minutes.
c) The half-life of the reaction is the time taken for half of the calcium carbonate to be used up.
    Calculate the half-life for this reaction.
d) Draw a rough graph to show how the volume of gas produced (y-axis) changes over the same period of time.

9. A student carried out a series of experiments to study the effect of changing the concentration of a reactant on the rate of the reaction. A plot of rate against relative concentration of the reactant produced the graph shown.

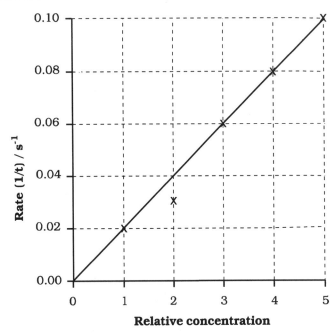

a) Predict the rate if the relative concentration had been increased to 8.
b) What time would have been recorded for the reaction with a relative concentration of 4?
c) The graph suggests that the time recorded for one of the experiments is wrong.
   Assuming the other points to be correct, what time should have been recorded for this experiment?

Exercise 1.2   Factors affecting rate

1. A piece of magnesium ribbon reacts with sulphuric acid to produce hydrogen and magnesium sulphate solution. If the magnesium is always covered by acid, state how you would expect the rate of production of hydrogen at the start of the reaction to be influenced by each of the following changes.
   a) using acid with a lower concentration
   b) using a greater volume of acid with the same concentration
   c) increasing the temperature of the reaction mixture
   d) using the same mass of powdered magnesium

2. Excess zinc powder was added to 100 cm^3 of sulphuric acid, concentration 2 mol l^{-1}, at room temperature. The volume of hydrogen produced was plotted against time.

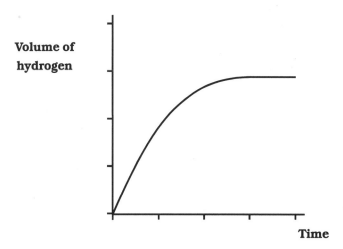

Copy the graph and add the corresponding curves which would be obtained if the reaction is repeated
   a) at a higher temperature,
   b) using zinc granules,
   c) using 100 cm^3 of hydrochloric acid, concentration 2 mol l^{-1},
   d) using 200 cm^3 of sulphuric acid, concentration 2 mol l^{-1}.
   (Label each curve clearly.)

3. Several experiments were carried out at room temperature with magnesium carbonate and acids. In each case 10 g (excess) of the carbonate was present at the start. The rate of mass loss was studied for various conditions.

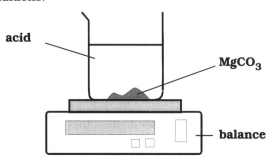

Experiment	Acid	$MgCO_3$
A	20 cm^3 HCl(aq), concentration 1 mol l^{-1}	Powdered
B	20 cm^3 HCl(aq), concentration 1 mol l^{-1}	Lump
C	20 cm^3 H$_2$SO$_4$(aq), concentration 1 mol l^{-1}	Powdered
D	10 cm^3 HCl(aq), concentration 1 mol l^{-1}	Powdered

The results of experiment **A** were plotted on a graph.

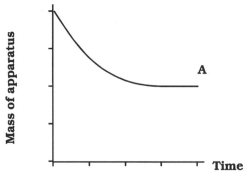

Copy the graph showing reaction **A** and add the corresponding curves which could have been obtained for experiments **B,C** and **D**.
(Label each curve clearly.)

Revision Questions for Higher Chemistry - Unit 1

4. The collision theory states that for two molecules to react, they must first collide with one another.

    a)   State **one** condition necessary for a reaction to follow from this collision.

    b)   Use the collision theory to explain the effect on reaction rate of the following changes.

        i)   increasing the concentration of reacting solutions

        ii) increasing the particle size of a solid

        iii) increasing the temperature

5. a)   Write balanced equations for the reaction of 1 mol of each of the following metals with an excess of dilute hydrochloric acid.

        i)   magnesium

        ii) zinc

        iii) sodium

   b)   The graph below shows how the volume of hydrogen produced as 0.1 mol of magnesium reacts with excess dilute hydrochloric acid varies with time.

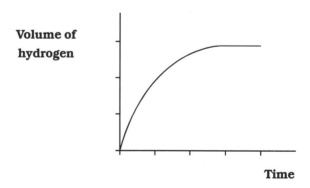

Copy this graph and add corresponding curves for the reactions of

    i)   0.1 mol of zinc (label this curve I),

    ii) 0.1 mol of sodium (label this curve II).

(Assume that the three metals have similar surface areas.)

6. Hydrogen peroxide solution decomposes to produce oxygen gas.

$$2H_2O_2(aq) \rightarrow 2H_2O(l) + O_2(g)$$

The rate of oxygen production was measured in three laboratory experiments using the same volume of hydrogen peroxide solution at the same temperature.

Experiment	Concentration of H_2O_2 / mol l^{-1}
A	0.2
B	0.4
C	0.1

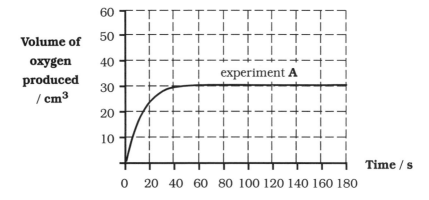

a) Copy the graph shown for experiment **A** and add curves to show the results of experiments **B** and **C**. Label each curve clearly.

b) In a fourth experiment **A** was repeated with the temperature increased by 20°C. State how this would affect
   i) the volume of oxygen produced in the first 20 s of the reaction,
   ii) the total volume of oxygen produced.

c) Draw a labelled diagram of assembled laboratory apparatus which could be used to carry out the experiment.

7. Carbon dioxide is produced when excess marble chips react with dilute hydrochloric acid.
   State **three** factors which would affect the rate of this chemical reaction.

8. The following graph shows the evolution of gas, with time, when two 0.5 g samples of calcium carbonate, each containing insoluble impurities, react with excess dilute hydrochloric acid.

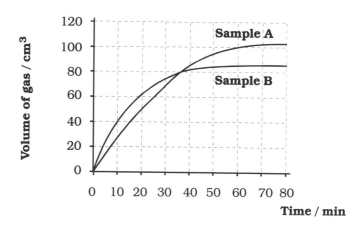

a) According to the graph, after what time does evolution of gas cease with sample **B**?
b) State which of the two samples has
    i)   the higher purity,
    ii) the smaller particle size.
c) Explain your answer to part b).

9. 1 g of magnesium is added to hydrochloric acid, concentration 0.5 mol l⁻¹. Using the same axes (volume of hydrogen evolved against time) sketch curves to show the differences you would expect for the reaction, given
    a) that magnesium is in excess,
    b) that the acid is in excess.
    (No graph paper is necessary.)

10. Hydrogen peroxide solution decomposes when heated.

$$2H_2O_2(aq) \rightarrow 2H_2O(l) + O_2(g)$$

The rates of decomposition of 100 cm^3 samples of each solution were followed under three different sets of conditions.

	Concentration of solution / %	Temperature of solution / °C
Curve 1	5.0	80
Curve 2	5.0	90
Curve 3	2.5	80

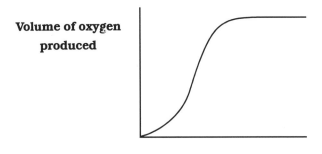

Volume of oxygen produced

Time

Copy the graph shown for curve 1 and add curves 2 and 3, corresponding to the different conditions.

11. The rates of many reactions are roughly doubled for a 10°C rise in temperature.

With the help of an energy distribution diagram, explain why a small temperature rise can have such a great effect on reaction rate.

12. In a "clock reaction" to study reaction rates, iodate ions in acid solution can be reduced to iodine by a solution of sulphite ions. Starch turns blue-black when iodine is formed and can be used as an indicator.

Two experiments were performed at room temperature. In each case, a solution of iodate ions was added to a solution containing sulphite ions and starch. The mixture was stirred and the time measured for the blue-black colour to appear.

Experiment 1

Volume of iodate solution / cm^3	Volume of water / cm^3	Volume of sulphite solution / cm^3	Time / s
25	40	15	13.8
20	45	15	17.0
15	50	15	24.8
10	55	15	35.5
5	60	15	68.7

Experiment 2

Volume of iodate solution / cm^3	Volume of water / cm^3	Volume of sulphite solution / cm^3	Time / s
25	25	30	5.8
20	30	30	8.0
15	35	30	10.0
10	40	30	13.5
5	45	30	24.5

a) In Experiment 1, which factor affects the reaction rate?

b) i) Compared with Experiment 1, which condition is altered in Experiment 2?

ii) What effect does this have on the reaction rate?

13. Sodium thiosulphate solution, $Na_2S_2O_3(aq)$, reacts with hydrochloric acid to produce a suspension of sulphur according to the equation.

$$S_2O_3{}^{2-}(aq) \quad + \quad 2H^+ \quad \rightarrow \quad S(s) \quad + \quad SO_2(g) \quad + \quad H_2O(l)$$

The rate of this reaction can be determined from the time it takes for the sulphur formed to obscure a cross marked on a sheet of paper underneath the reaction vessel.

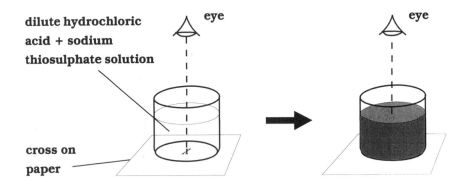

A pupil carried out a series of experiments to study the effect of the concentration of sodium thiosulphate solution on the rate of reaction and obtained the following results.

	Volume of $Na_2S_2O_3(aq)$ used / cm^3	Volume of water added / cm^3	Relative concentration of $Na_2S_2O_3(aq)$	Volume of HCl(aq) added / cm^3	Time (t) for X to vanish / s	Rate (1/t) / s^{-1}
A	50	0	5	10	10.0	0.10
B	40	10	4	10	12.5	0.08
C	30	20	3	10	16.7	0.06
D	20	30	2	10	33.3	0.03
E	10	40	1	10	50.0	0.02

a) From the first two columns of the results table, which factor is being kept constant throughout the series of experiments?

b) i) What conclusion can be drawn concerning the concentration of the thiosulphate solution and the reaction rate?

ii) Explain why changing the concentration affects the reaction rate.

c) State **one** other way of increasing the rate of this reaction.

14. Three experiments were carried out in a study of the rate of reaction between magnesium (in excess) and dilute hydrochloric acid. A balance was used to record the mass of the reaction flask and its contents. The results of Experiment 1, using magnesium ribbon and 0.4 mol l^{-1} acid are shown in the graph.

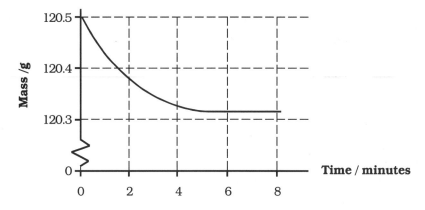

a) Why did the balance record a decrease in mass during the reaction?

b) The only difference between Experiment 2 and Experiment 1 was the use of magnesium powder.
Copy the above graph and sketch a curve that could be expected for Experiment 2. (Label it 2)

c) The only difference between Experiment 3 and Experiment 1 was the use of 0.2 mol l^{-1} acid.
On the graph, sketch a curve that could be expected for Experiment 3. (Label it 3)

Exercise 1.3   Mole calculations

1. Calculate the mass of each of the following compounds.
   a)   10 mol of CH_4
   b)   0.5 mol of SO_2
   c)   2 mol of Na_2CO_3
   d)   0.1 mol of $(NH_4)_2Cr_2O_7$

2. Calculate the amount, in moles, in each of the following compounds.
   a)   10 g of $CaCO_3$
   b)   14 g of C_2H_4
   c)   202 g of KNO_3
   d)   6.6 g of $(NH_4)_2SO_4$

3. Calculate the amount, in moles, which must be dissolved to make each of the following solutions.
   a)   200 cm^3 of 1 mol l^{-1}
   b)   500 cm^3 of 0.5 mol l^{-1}
   c)   100 cm^3 of 2 mol l^{-1}
   d)   2 litres of 0.2 mol l^{-1}

4. Calculate the concentration of each of the following solutions.
   a)   1 mol of solute dissolved in 500 cm^3 of solution
   b)   2 mol of solute dissolved in 200 cm^3 of solution
   c)   0.5 mol of solute dissolved in 250 cm^3 of solution
   d)   0.1 mol of solute dissolved in 1 litre of solution

5. Calculate the volume of each of the following solutions.
   a)   1 mol l^{-1} solution containing 2 mol of solute
   b)   2 mol l^{-1} solution containing 0.4 mol of solute
   c)   0.5 mol l^{-1} solution containing 0.1 mol of solute
   d)   1 mol l^{-1} solution containing 0.2 mol of solute

6. Calculate the mass of substance required to make up each of the following solutions.

   a)   50 cm^3 of 4 mol l^{-1} KCl(aq)

   b)   100 cm^3 of 0.2 mol l^{-1} Na$_2$SO$_4$(aq)

   c)   25 cm^3 of 1 mol l^{-1} Mg(NO$_3$)$_2$(aq)

   d)   500 cm^3 of 0.1 mol l^{-1} (NH$_4$)$_2$CO$_3$(aq)

7. Calculate the concentration of each of the following solutions.

   a)   4 g of NaOH dissolved in 1 litre of solution

   b)   13.8 g of K$_2$CO$_3$ dissolved in 2 litres of solution

   c)   16 g of CuSO$_4$ dissolved in 250 cm^3 of solution

   d)   10 g of NH$_4$NO$_3$ dissolved in 100 cm^3 of solution

Exercise 1.4   Calculations based on equations

1. a) CH_4 + $2O_2$ → CO_2 + $2H_2O$

    Calculate the mass of carbon dioxide which is produced on burning
    4 g of methane.

    b) $2Mg$ + O_2 → $2MgO$

    Calculate the mass of magnesium which is required to produce
    5 g of magnesium oxide.

    c) C_2H_4 + H_2O → C_2H_5OH (ethanol)

    Calculate the mass of ethanol which is produced from
    10^3 kg of ethene.

    d) N_2 + $3H_2$ → $2NH_3$

    Calculate the mass of ammonia which is produced from
    6 tonnes of hydrogen assuming 80% efficiency.

    e) $CH_3CH_2CH_2OH$ → CH_3CH_2COOH
                  propan-1-ol   propanoic acid

    Calculate the mass of propan-1-ol which would give
    1.48 kg of propanoic acid assuming 60% conversion.

2. a) 25 cm^3 of hydrochloric acid, concentration 1 mol l^{-1}, required
    50 cm^3 of sodium hydroxide solution for complete neutralisation.
    Calculate the concentration of the sodium hydroxide solution.

    b) Calculate the volume of sulphuric acid, concentration 2 mol l^{-1},
    required to neutralise 25 cm^3 of sodium hydroxide solution,
    concentration 1 mol l^{-1}.

    c) 12.8 cm^3 of potassium hydroxide solution is neutralised by 25 cm^3
    of nitric acid, concentration 0.22 mol l^{-1}.
    Calculate the concentration of the potassium hydroxide solution.

3. Trichloromethane is insoluble in water. When ammonia is added to a beaker containing water and trichloromethane, the ammonia dissolves in both solvents giving different concentrations.

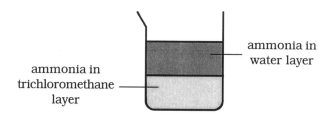

ammonia in water layer

ammonia in trichloromethane layer

The ratio

$$\frac{\text{concentration of ammonia in water}}{\text{concentration of ammonia in trichloromethane}}$$

is called the partition coefficient.

This can be found by titrating the ammonia in each layer against dilute hydrochloric acid.

The concentration of ammonia in water was found to be 1.7 mol l^{-1}. For the ammonia in trichloromethane, it was found that 18.4 cm^3 of dilute hydrochloric acid, concentration 0.050 mol l^{-1} was required to neutralise 20.0 cm^3 of the ammonia solution.

Calculate the value for the partition coefficient of ammonia between water and trichloromethane.

4. A chemist was investigating the mass of calcium carbonate present in different egg shells.

It was found that the calcium carbonate in one of the egg shell samples reacted with 50.10 cm^3 of hydrochloric acid, concentration 1 mol l^{-1}.

Calculate the mass of calcium carbonate present in the egg shell sample.

Exercise 1.5   The idea of excess

1. In each of the reactions, decide by calculation which reactant is in excess.
    a) 6.5 g of zinc added to 25 cm^3 of dilute sulphuric acid,
        concentration 2 mol l^{-1}
    b) 2.4 g of magnesium added to 100 cm^3 of dilute hydrochloric acid,
        concentration 1 mol l^{-1}
    c) 3.6 g of zinc added to 50 cm^3 of dilute hydrochloric acid,
        concentration 0.5 mol l^{-1}
    d) 4.7 g of magnesium added to 25 cm^3 of dilute sulphuric acid,
        concentration 1 mol l^{-1}

2. Calculate the mass of magnesium oxide which is obtained when 0.24 g of
    magnesium is burned in 0.25 mol of oxygen.

3. Calculate the mass of water which is obtained when 0.2 g of hydrogen is
    ignited with 0.1 mol of oxygen.

4. $(NH_4)_2SO_4$ + $2NaOH$ → $2NH_3$ + Na_2SO_4 + $2H_2O$
    Calculate the mass of ammonia gas which is produced when 1.32 g of
    ammonium sulphate is heated with 1 g of sodium hydroxide.

5. $Na_2SO_3(s)$ + $2HCl(aq)$ → $2NaCl(aq)$ + $H_2O(l)$ + $SO_2(g)$
    Calculate the mass of sulphur dioxide produced when 1.26 g of sodium
    sulphite is added to 50 cm^3 of dilute hydrochloric acid,
    concentration 2 mol l^{-1}.

6. Calculate the mass of hydrogen gas which is produced when 5 g of zinc is
    added to 100 cm^3 of dilute hydrochloric acid, concentration 2 mol l^{-1}.

7. Calculate the mass of carbon dioxide which is obtained when 0.1 g of
    methane is ignited with 0.5 g of oxygen.

Revision Questions for Higher Chemistry - Unit 1

Exercise 1.6   Catalysts

1. The equation below represents the catalytic oxidation of ammonia.

    $$4NH_3(g) \quad + \quad 5O_2(g) \quad \rightarrow \quad 4NO(g) \quad + \quad 6H_2O(g)$$

    a) i) Why is the catalyst used in the form of a fine wire mesh?
        ii) What would be the products if no catalyst were used?
    b) The catalyst used in this reaction is an example of a heterogeneous catalyst.
        What is meant by heterogeneous?

2. Hydrogen, for use in the Haber Process, can be produced by the reaction:

    pentane + water $\rightarrow$ carbon monoxide + hydrogen

    The carbon monoxide formed must be removed or it will poison the catalyst used in the Haber Process.
    a) Explain how the catalyst works.
    b) Why is the catalyst spread out?
    c) What happens when the catalyst is poisoned?

3. When heated, an aqueous mixture of sodium potassium tartrate and hydrogen peroxide produces oxygen slowly. When a cobalt salt is present in the original mixture, the solution is pink. On warming, oxygen is released rapidly and the colour changes to green. As the effervescence subsides, the colour changes to pink again.
    a) Explain these changes in terms of catalysis.
    b) What kind of catalyst is involved in the reaction?

4. The breakdown of fats to form fatty acids in the small intestine is catalysed by a naturally occurring organic substance called lipase.
    a) What name is given to organic catalysts such as lipase?
    b) Give **one** other naturally-occurring reaction catalysed by an organic catalyst and name the catalyst involved.

5. To reduce the pollutants in exhaust fumes, more and more cars are being fitted with catalytic converters. A typical converter has a honeycomb structure through which the exhaust gases pass. Metal catalysts such as platinum, rhodium and palladium are distributed through the honeycomb.

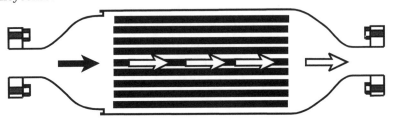

a) Explain why the converter has a honeycomb structure.
b) As what kind of catalysts are the metals acting?
c) Give **one** reaction which is catalysed by a catalytic converter.
d) Explain why "leaded" petrol is not recommended for use with a catalytic converter.

6. Give **one** example of
a) a catalyst used in an industrial process and the reaction which it catalyses,
b) an enzyme used in an industrial process and the reaction which it catalyses.

7. The graph shows the volume of oxygen produced by the decomposition of hydrogen peroxide under normal conditions.

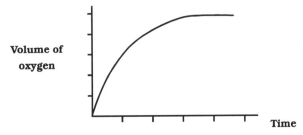

Copy the graph and add a second curve to show the results that you would expect to obtain if the experiment was repeated with the only change being the addition of a catalyst.

Exercise 1.7   Potential energy diagrams

1. a) What is meant by an exothermic reaction?
    b) What is meant by an endothermic reaction?

2. $H_2(g)$ + $I_2(g)$ ⇌ $2HI(g)$

    The activation energy for the forward reaction is 181.5 kJ mol^{-1} and for
    the reverse reaction is 192.8 kJ mol^{-1}.
    a) What is the enthalpy change for the forward reaction?
    b) Is the forward reaction exothermic or endothermic?

3. The potential energy diagram refers to an industrial reaction:

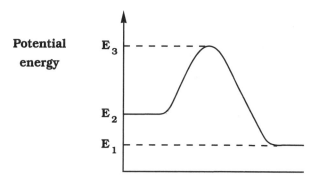

Reaction pathway

    a) In terms of E_1, E_2, and E_3, state
        i)   the activation energy for the forward reaction,
        ii) the enthalpy change for the reverse reaction.
    b) State the effect a catalyst would have on
        i)   the activation energy for the forward reaction,
        ii) the enthalpy change for the reaction.

4. Inhibitors can be thought of as negative catalysts. They are commonly
    added to plastics to slow down thermal degradation.
    For the degradation reaction, state the effect of such inhibitors on
    a) the enthalpy change,
    b) the activation energy.

5. Consider the following potential energy diagram.

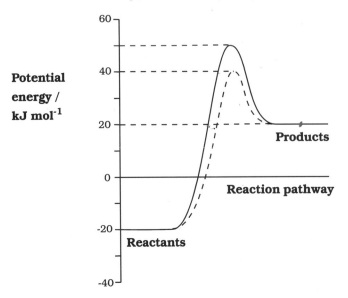

a) State the value of the activation energy for
    i) the uncatalysed forward reaction,
    ii) the uncatalysed reverse reaction,
    iii) the catalysed forward reaction,
    iv) the catalysed reverse reaction.
b) State the value for the enthalpy change for
    i) the forward reaction,
    ii) the reverse reaction.

6. The activation energy (E_A) and the enthalpy change (ΔH) for the reaction of nitrogen with hydrogen to form ammonia are 236 kJ mol^{-1} and −92kJ mol^{-1} respectively.
a) Present this information on graph paper to show the potential energy diagram for the reaction.
b) Calculate the activation energy for the reverse reaction.

7.   The diagram shows the energy changes involved in an uncatalysed reaction and also in the catalysed (faster) reaction.

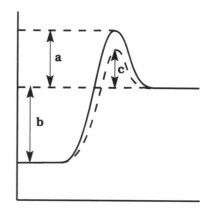

Potential energy

Reaction pathway

a)   State the value (in terms of **a**, **b**, and **c**) of

   i)   the activation energy of the uncatalysed forward reaction,

   ii)   the activation energy of the catalysed reverse reaction,

   iii)   the enthalpy change for the forward reaction.

b)   Is the forward reaction exothermic or endothermic?

8.   The following potential energy diagram refers to the uncatalysed decomposition of hydrogen peroxide.

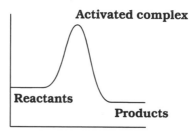

Potential energy

Activated complex

Reactants

Products

Reaction pathway

a)   Copy the potential energy diagram and add a curve to represent the decomposition when catalase, a catalyst, is added to the hydrogen peroxide solution.

b)   What is meant by the activated complex?

Exercise 1.8   Enthalpy changes

1. a) Write the balanced chemical equation corresponding to
        i)   the enthalpy of combustion of methanol,
        ii) the enthalpy of solution of potassium hydroxide.
    b) Write the ion equation corresponding to the enthalpy of
        neutralisation of hydrochloric acid by an alkali.

2. An experiment was carried out using the apparatus shown.

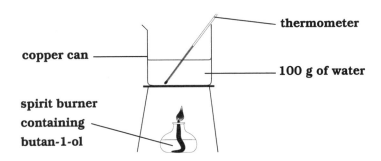

    By measuring the temperature rise of the water and the change in mass
    of the spirit burner, it was found that 0.6 g of butan-1-ol burned to give
    out 8.36 kJ of energy.
    a) Use these values to calculate a value for the enthalpy of combustion
        of butan-1-ol.
    b) Why is the answer calculated in part a) different from the value given
        in your data booklet, assuming that the mass and temperature
        measurements above are accurate?

3. When 1 g of ethanol was burned, the heat produced warmed 5 litres of
    water from 20.1 °C to 21.5 °C.
    Calculate the enthalpy of combustion of ethanol.

4. When 1 g of sulphur was completely burned in air, the heat produced
    warmed 110 g of water from 18 °C to 38 °C.
    Calculate the enthalpy of combustion of sulphur.

5.   The enthalpies of combustion of methanol, ethanol and propanol are
     -726, -1370 and -2020 kJ mol^{-1} respectively.
     a)   i)   Why is there a regular increase in enthalpies of combustion from
               methanol to ethanol to propanol?
          ii) Estimate the enthalpy of combustion of butanol.
     b)   Calculate the amount of heat liberated by the complete combustion of
          1.0 g of propanol.
     c)   Dimethyl ether (CH_3-O-CH_3) has the same molecular formula as
          ethanol.
          Why then does it have a different enthalpy of combustion?

6.   When 11.9 g of potassium bromide was dissolved in water, the amount of
     heat absorbed was 2.1 kJ.
     Calculate the enthalpy of solution of potassium bromide.

7.   A pupil read in a text book that sodium hydroxide had an enthalpy of
     solution of -42.7 kJ mol^{-1}. He decided to check this by experiment.

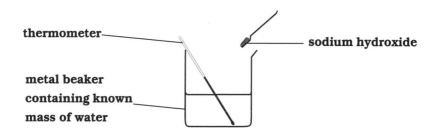

thermometer

sodium hydroxide

metal beaker
containing known
mass of water

He dissolved 20 g of sodium hydroxide in water and measured the
temperature increase. He calculated from this that the amount of heat
produced in the reaction was 19.8 kJ.
     a)   Use the pupil's results to calculate the enthalpy of solution of sodium
          hydroxide.
     b)   Explain why the enthalpy of solution calculated in a) is different from
          the textbook value.
     c)   Describe an improvement which could be made to this experiment to
          achieve a result closer to the textbook value.

8. When 2 g of a compound (relative formula mass 40) is dissolved in 50 cm^3 of water, the temperature rises by 10 °C.
    Calculate the enthalpy of solution of the compound.

9. In a laboratory experiment, 10 g of ammonium nitrate, NH_4NO_3, was dissolved in 400 cm^3 of water.
    Calculate the change in temperature of the solution.
    (Take the enthalpy of solution of ammonium nitrate to be + 26 kJ mol^{-1}.)

10. When 100 cm^3 of dilute nitric acid, concentration 0.1 mol l^{-1}, is neutralised by sodium hydroxide solution, 570 J of heat is liberated.
    Calculate the enthalpy of neutralisation of nitric acid.

11. The following results are taken from the notebook of a pupil.

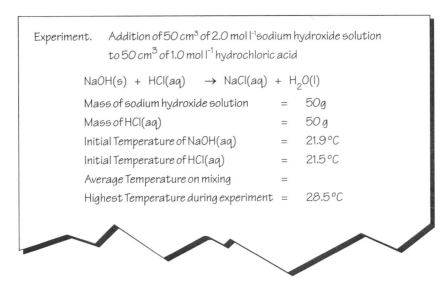

Experiment. Addition of 50 cm³ of 2.0 mol l⁻¹ sodium hydroxide solution
             to 50 cm³ of 1.0 mol l⁻¹ hydrochloric acid

NaOH(s) + HCl(aq)   → NaCl(aq) + H₂O(l)

Mass of sodium hydroxide solution	=	50g
Mass of HCl(aq)	=	50 g
Initial Temperature of NaOH(aq)	=	21.9 °C
Initial Temperature of HCl(aq)	=	21.5 °C
Average Temperature on mixing	=	
Highest Temperature during experiment	=	28.5 °C

Calculate the enthalpy of neutralisation of hydrochloric acid by sodium hydroxide solution.

Exercise 1.9   Atomic and ionic size

1. a) Draw a graph of atomic size (y-axis) against atomic number for the
        elements 3 to 20, using information from your data booklet.
        (Use a dotted line between atomic numbers 9 and 11, and
        17 and 19.)
    b) What evidence is there to support the idea that the atomic size is
        a periodic property?

2. a) Explain the change in atomic size of atoms of the elements
        i)   on crossing the Periodic Table from lithium to fluorine,
        ii) on going down Group I from lithium to caesium.
    b) State whereabouts in the Periodic Table you would expect to find
        elements with
        i)   the smallest atomic size,
        ii) the largest atomic size.

3. Explain why
    a) the sodium atom is larger than the chlorine atom,
    b) the sodium ion is smaller than the chloride ion.

4. For each pair of ions given below, explain why the first mentioned ion has
    a greater size than the second.
    a) Na^+ and Mg^{2+}
    b) Ca^{2+} and Mg^{2+}
    c) F^- and Na^+

5. The graph below relates the ionic size of some elements to their atomic numbers.

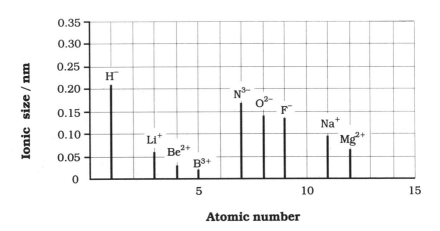

Atomic number

a) State the ionic sizes you would predict for the ions of the elements with atomic numbers 13 and 15.

b) The value quoted above for hydrogen is for the hydride ion (H^-).
   i) Why is no value given for the H^+ ion?
   ii) Why is the H^- ion larger than the Li^+ ion?

c) Why is there a large increase in size from boron to nitrogen?

6. On crossing the Periodic Table there are trends in the sizes of atoms and ions.

a) Explain why the ions of sodium, magnesium, aluminium and silicon are much smaller than their corresponding atoms.

b) Explain why there is a large increase in ionic size from silicon to phosphorus.

c) What do all the ions from nitrogen, N^{3-}, to silicon, Si^{4+}, have in common?

d) Explain why the ionic sizes tend to decrease along this sequence from nitrogen to silicon.

Exercise 1.10   Ionisation energy and electronegativity

1. a) What is meant by the first ionisation energy of an element?
    b) i)   Is the process involved exothermic or endothermic?
        ii) Explain your answer.
    c) Write equations corresponding to the first ionisation energies of sodium and calcium.
    d) Refer to your data booklet and alongside each of the above equations write in the ΔH value with its appropriate sign.

2. a) Write an equation corresponding to
        i)   the second ionisation energy of magnesium,
        ii) the third ionisation energy of aluminium.
    b) Refer to your data booklet and alongside each of the above equations write in the ΔH value with its appropriate sign.

3. a) Using the information in your data booklet, draw a graph of the first ionisation energy (y-axis) against atomic number for the first twenty elements. (Use a dotted line between the noble gases and the elements in Group 1.)
    b) Explain why the first ionisation energy can be described as a periodic property.

4. a) Explain the trend in first ionisation energies on going down the Group 1 metals:

        lithium   →   sodium   →   potassium
    b) Explain the difference between the first and second ionisation energies of these elements.
    c) Why is there no value given in the data booklet for the fourth ionisation energy of lithium?

5. Explain the trend in the first ionisation energies on going across the Periodic Table:

        sodium   →   magnesium   →   aluminium

6. Look at the table of ionisation energies in your data booklet.
    a) Explain the difference between the first ionisation energy of each alkali metal and that of the halogen in the same period.
    b) Explain the difference between the second ionisation energy of each alkali metal and that of the halogen in the same period.

7. Calculate the energy required to bring about the following changes:
    a) $Al(g)$ $\rightarrow$ $Al^{3+}(g)$
    b) $K^{+}(g)$ $\rightarrow$ $K^{3+}(g)$

8. a) Which **three** elements (in the first 20) have the lowest first ionisation energies?
    b) In which group are these elements?
    c) Explain why these elements have the lowest first ionisation energies.

9. The following table shows approximate ionisation energies, in kJ mol^{-1}, of five elements, **A, B, C, D** and **E**.

Element	1st I.E.	2nd I.E.	3rd I.E.	4th I.E.
A	520	7300	11500	-
B	2100	3900	6100	9400
C	580	1800	2800	11500
D	740	1450	7700	10500
E	420	3050	4500	5900

State which of these elements
a) will be in Group 2 of the Periodic Table,
b) will be in the same group of the Periodic Table,
c) will be the least reactive.
d) would require the least energy to convert one mole of gaseous atoms into ions carrying three positive charges.

10. a) Which **two** elements (in the first 20) have the highest first ionisation energies?
    b) In which group are these elements?
    c) Explain why these elements have the highest first ionisation energies.

11. a) Which elements show the greatest difference between their first ionisation energies and their second ionisation energies.
    b) Explain your answer.

12. Explain the difference between the third ionisation energy of magnesium and that of aluminium.

13. The diagram shows the first ionisation energies of successive elements **A** to **T**, plotted against their atomic numbers.

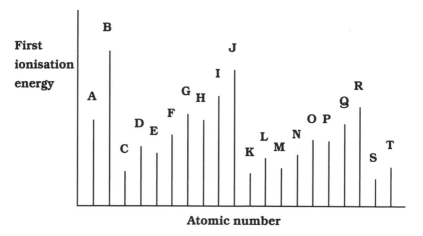

a) Which group of elements is represented by the letters **B**, **J** and **R**?
b) State which elements can be identified as
   i) halogens,
   ii) alkali metals.
c) Why is the first ionisation energy of element **L** greater than that of element **K**?
d) Why is the second ionisation energy of element **L** considerably less than that of element **K**?

14. Ionisation energies can be found by applying an increasing voltage across test samples of gases until the gases ionise.

    The results below were obtained from experiments using hydrogen atoms and then helium atoms.

Element	Voltage at which an atom of gas ionises / V	
hydrogen	13.6	no further change
helium	24.6	54.5

a) Why are there two results for helium but only one for hydrogen?

b) Why is the first ionisation energy of helium higher than that of hydrogen?

15. a) Using the information in your data booklet, draw a graph of electronegativity (y-axis) against atomic number for the first twenty elements. (Use a dotted line between the noble gases and the elements in Group 1.)

b) Explain why electronegativity can be described as a periodic property.

16. a) Explain the trend in electronegativity values on going down the Group 7 elements:

    fluorine → chlorine → bromine

b) Explain the trend in electronegativity values on going across the Periodic Table:

    sodium → magnesium → aluminium

c) Which group in the Periodic Table has elements with no quoted values for electronegativity?

Exercise 1.11   Types of bonding and structure

1. Taking hydrogen sulphide as an example, describe what happens in the formation of a covalent bond.

2. a) Using hydrogen fluoride as an example, explain how a polar covalent bond arises.
   b) i) Which is the more polar bond, H–F or H–Cl?
      ii) Explain your answer.

3. a) For the formation of a metal ion (gas phase) from a metal atom (solid) is the process endothermic or exothermic?
   b) i) What happens during the formation of an ionic bond?
      ii) Is the process endothermic or exothermic?

4. hydrogen oxide, chlorine, sodium fluoride, fluorine, potassium chloride, nitrogen chloride, oxygen, lithium oxide, hydrogen sulphide.

   From the above list, name the substances which are best described as
   a) pure covalent,
   b) polar covalent,
   c) ionic.

5. Explain why ammonia, NH_3, has polar covalent bonds yet nitrogen and hydrogen do not.

6. Explain why carbon disulphide contains pure covalent bonds.

7. a) Which two elements in the second period will form the compound with most ionic character.
   b) Give a reason for your choice.

8. Explain why you would expect rubidium fluoride to be the most ionic of the halides of rubidium.

9. What is meant by metallic bonding?

10. Silicon oxide has a covalent network structure;
    sulphur dioxide consists of disrete molecules.
    a) What is meant by a covalent network structure?
    b) Name the type of bonds (or forces) which are broken at the melting point of
        i)   silicon oxide,
        ii) sulphur dioxide.

11. Name the type of bonds which are broken at the melting point of
    a) sodium,
    b) sodium chloride.

Exercise 1.12   Intermolecular forces of attraction

1. a) What is meant by van der Waals' forces?
    b) What causes these forces?
    c) What is the trend in the strength of van der Waals' forces going down Group 7?

2. a) How do the strengths of the forces involved in hydrogen bonding compare with the strengths of the van der Waals' forces?

    b) How do the strengths of the forces involved in hydrogen bonding compare with the strengths of covalent bonds?

3. H_2, HF, NCl_3, Cl_2, H_2O, PF_3, N_2, HBr, NH_3

    Copy the table below and place each of the above formulae in the correct column.

Van der Waals forces occur; no permanent dipole - permanent dipole interactions; no hydrogen bonding	Permanent dipole - permanent dipole interactions occur; no hydrogen bonding	Hydrogen bonding occurs

4. Explain why ammonia, NH_3, exhibits a high degree of hydrogen bonding, yet there is no such bonding in hydrogen gas.

5. Analysis of hydrogen fluoride shows the existence of molecules with relative molecular masses of 20, 40 and 60.
    Explain the origin of these molecules.

Exercise 1.13   Polarity of molecules

1. Explain the difference between a polar molecule and a polar bond.

2. By drawing the shape and considering the symmetry, decide whether or
    not each of the following molecules is polar.
    a) ammonia (NH_3)   b) methane (CH_4)
    c) chloroform ($CHCl_3$)   d) silicon tetrachloride ($SiCl_4$)

3. The bonds in both water and carbon dioxide are polar.
    Why is water a polar substance but carbon dioxide is a non-polar
    substance?

4. A jet of water from a burette is deflected when a charged rod is held close
    to it. Other liquids treated a similar way gave the following results.

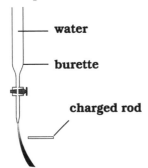

Group A	Group B
water	cyclohexane
propanone	benzene
ethanol	pentane
trichloromethane	

a) Why are the liquids in group **A** deflected but those in group **B** are
    not?
b) Explain what would happen with a jet of tetrachloromethane.

5. The benzene ring is a symmetrical arrangement of carbon and hydrogen
    atoms. The hydrogen atoms can be replaced by other atoms, eg chlorine.
    Two dichlorobenzene isomers are shown.

 represents the
benzene ring

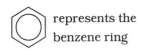

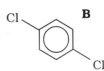

Why is molecule **A** polar while molecule **B** is not polar?

Exercise 1.14   Bonding and structure - the elements

1.   From the first twenty elements, name an element made up of
      a)   diatomic molecules with a single bond between the atoms,
      b)   diatomic molecules with a double covalent bond between the atoms,
      c)   diatomic molecules with a triple covalent bond between the atoms,
      d)   four atom molecules,
      e)   eight atom molecules.

2.   Draw a diagram to show the structure of
      a)   diamond,
      b)   graphite.

3.   State what is meant by
      a)   a covalent network of atoms,
      b)   a discrete molecule,
      c)   a monatomic gas.

4.   a)   State what is meant by delocalised electrons in a metal.
      b)   Explain why metals are good electrical conductors both as solids and
            liquids.

5.   New forms of carbon have recently been made. They exist as individual
      molecules of different sizes and are called fullerenes. The main fullerene
      has the formula C_{60}.
      How does the structure of a fullerene differ from that of diamond?

6.   State the type of bonding which exists in
      a)   fluorine,
      b)   sulphur,
      c)   aluminium,
      d)   silicon.

7.

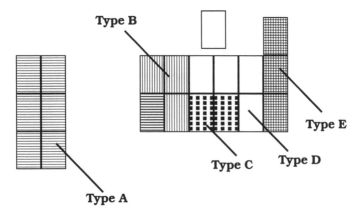

Type B

Type E

Type C   Type D

Type A

Copy and complete the table by adding the appropriate letter for each of the following types of element.

Type	Bonding and structure at normal room temperature and pressure
	Monatomic gases
	Covalent network solids
	Diatomic covalent gases
	Discrete covalent molecular solids
	Metallic lattice solids

Exercise 1.15   Properties of substances

1. Compound **X** has a melting point of 1700 °C and does not conduct electricity when molten.

    a) State the type of bonding and structure which exist in compound **X**.

    b) Explain your answer.

2.

	Melting point / °C	Boiling point / °C
Sodium chloride	801	1417
Carbon tetrachloride	–23	77

From the above information, a pupil deduced that ionic bonding must be stronger than covalent bonding.
Explain whether or not you agree with this conclusion.

3. Titanium chloride, $TiCl_4$, is a colourless liquid which boils at 132 °C. Explain whether the bonding in titanium chloride is likely to be ionic or covalent.

4. The table shows the melting points of lithium halides.

Halide	M.pt. / °C
LiF	842
LiCl	614
LiBr	547
LiI	450

Explain the trend in melting points.

5. Explain why phosphorus trichloride has a melting point of –91°C but sodium chloride has a melting point of 801°C.

6. Explain why the boiling points of the halogens increase on going down the group from fluorine to bromine.

7. The diagram illustrates the trend in the boiling points of the Group 7 hydrides, HCl, HBr and HI.

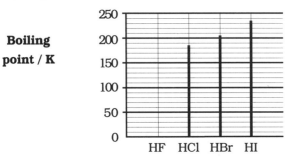

a) Why is the boiling point of HI higher than that of HBr?
b) Estimate the boiling point of hydrogen fluoride, HF, **if it were to follow this trend.**
c) The actual boiling point of HF is 292 K.
    Account for this unexpectedly high value.

8.

Compound	Formula	Molecular mass	Boiling point / °C
ethane	CH_3CH_3	30	–89
methanol	CH_3OH	32	64
hydrazine	NH_2NH_2	32	113
silane	SiH_4	32	–112

a) From the information given, which of the compounds in the table contain hydrogen bonding in the liquid state?
b) Why does hydrogen bonding affect the boiling point of a substance?
c) The table compares substances of similar molecular mass.
    Why is molecular mass significant in this case?
d) State **two** other ways in which the presence of hydrogen bonding could affect the physical properties of a substance.

9. Liquid ammonia boils at –33 °C but liquid phosphine, PH_3, boils at –87.5 °C.
    Explain this difference in terms of bonding.

10. Explain why the boiling point of hydrogen peroxide, H_2O_2 (150 °C), is much higher than that of hydrogen sulphide, H_2S (– 61 °C), which has the same molecular mass.

11.

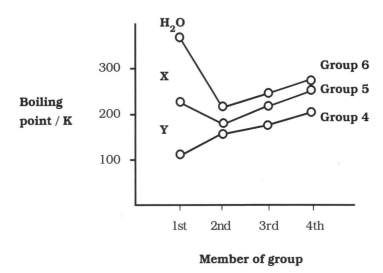

The graph shows the boiling points of the hydrides of elements in Groups 4, 5 and 6 of the Periodic Table.

a) Identify compounds **X** and **Y**.

b) Why is there a fairly steady increase in the boiling points of the Group 4 hydrides on going down the group?

c) What causes water and compound **X** to have boiling points considerably higher than expected?

12.

$$\begin{array}{c} H \quad\; H \; H \\ | \quad\;\; | \; \; | \\ H-C-O-C-C-H \\ | \quad\;\; | \; \; | \\ H \quad\; H \; H \end{array}$$

methoxyethane

$$\begin{array}{c} H \; H \; H \\ | \; \; | \; \; | \\ H-C-C-C-O-H \\ | \; \; | \; \; | \\ H \; H \; H \end{array}$$

propan-1-ol

Predict which of the above isomers will have the higher boiling point and explain your choice.

13. Arrange the molecules below in order of increasing viscosity.

$$CH_3-CH_2-OH$$

$$\begin{matrix} CH_2-CH-CH_2 \\ | \quad | \quad | \\ OH \quad OH \quad OH \end{matrix}$$

$$\begin{matrix} CH_2-CH_2 \\ | \quad | \\ OH \quad OH \end{matrix}$$

ethanol   **propan-1,2,3-triol**   **ethan-1,2-diol**

14. A pupil is comparing the boiling points of alkanes and alkanols to examine the influence of hydrogen bonding.
    a) Why do the boiling points of the alkanes increase with increasing molecular mass?
    b) Which of the two families has hydrogen bonding between the molecules?
    c) i) To examine the influence of hydrogen bonding, the boiling point of which alkane should be compared with that of butane?
       ii) Explain your answer.

15. Maleic acid and fumaric acid have the same molecular formula. Their structures are different because rotation is not possible about the carbon-carbon double bond.

maleic acid
m.pt. 157 °C

fumaric acid
m.pt. 287 °C

    a) The molecular mass of octane (melting point –57 °C) is the same as that of the two acids.
       Why is its melting point lower than the melting point of the acids?
    b) Why is the melting point of fumaric acid higher than that of maleic acid?

16. a) Explain why diamond is hard and is a non-conductor of electricity.
    b) Explain why graphite is soft and is a conductor of electricity.
    c) Explain why graphite is an effective lubricant.

17. a) Explain why the covalent network elements have very high melting points.
    b) Explain why elements made up of discrete molecules have relatively low melting and boiling points.

18.

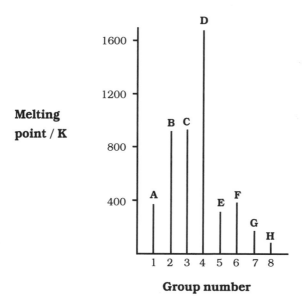

Group number

The graph shows the melting points for the elements across a period in the Periodic Table.
a) Identify the period represented by the graph.
b) The bonding in both elements **A** and **B** is metallic.
   Explain why the melting point of element **B** is higher than that of element **A**.
c) Elements **D** and **E** are both covalently bonded.
   In terms of structure account for the large difference in their melting points.

19. Use a data booklet to find the melting points of chlorine, phosphorus, magnesium and silicon.
    a) Explain why the melting points of chlorine and phosphorus are low.
    b) Explain why the melting points of magnesium and silicon are high.

20. a) Using a data booklet, state the melting point of
        i) lithium,
        ii) sodium,
        iii) potassium.
    b) i) Going down the group from lithium to sodium state what must happen to the strength of the metallic bonds.
       ii) Explain why this happens.

21. Explain each of the following.
    a) Potassium chloride dissolves readily in water but not in cyclohexane.
    b) Tetrachloromethane dissolves in hexane but not in water.

22. Lithium iodide is moderately soluble in non-polar solvents whereas caesium chloride is not.
    On the basis of this evidence deduce the difference in bonding in the two compounds

23. Taking sodium chloride as your example, explain, in terms of bonding, what happens to an ionic crystal when it dissolves in water.

24. In the second period, the melting points of boron and carbon are much higher than the melting points of nitrogen, oxygen and fluorine.
    Explain why this is so.

25. Methanol, CH_3OH, can be used as an alternative fuel in car engines.
    It is less volatile than petrol and less likely to explode in a car accident.
    Explain why methanol is less volatile than petrol.

26. The table shows the melting points and boiling points of the chlorides in the first period.

Chloride	LiCl	$BeCl_2$	BCl_3	CCl_4	NCl_3	OCl_2	FCl
M.pt. / °C	614	405	−107	−23	−27	−20	−154
B.pt. / °C	1350	487	12	77	71	4	−101

a) Which chloride is a gas at 0 °C?
b) Which chloride is a typical ionic solid?
c) Which chloride is most likely to be a covalent solid at room temperature?
d) i) What happens to the polarity of the **X**–Cl bond as one progresses across the table from left to right?
   ii) Explain your answer.

27.

Substance	Melting point / °C	Boiling point / °C	Electrical conductivity of solid	Electrical conductivity of melt
A	92	190	nil	nil
B	1053	2500	good	good
C	773	1407	nil	good
D	1883	2503	nil	nil

Place **A**, **B**, **C** and **D** in the appropriate category.
Choose from the following:
ionic, covalent network, covalent discrete molecular, metallic.

28. Laundry bags, used in hospitals, are made from poly(ethenol), a polymer which will dissolve in hot or cold water. Poly(ethenol) has the following structure.

Explain why poly(ethenol) is soluble in water but poly(ethene) is insoluble in water.

29. Tin iodide can be prepared directly from its elements.

Excess tin is heated for about an hour with iodine dissolved in tetrachloromethane.

Tetrachloromethane, which has a boiling point of 77 °C, acts as a solvent both for iodine and for the tin iodide that is formed.

When the reaction is complete, the excess tin is removed. On cooling the remaining solution, orange crystals of tin iodide appear.

The crystals have a melting point of 144 °C.

Give **two** pieces of evidence from the method of preparation which suggest that tin iodide is a discrete molecular covalent compound.

Exercise 1.16   The Avogadro Constant

1. Calculate the amount, in moles, in each of the following compounds.
   a) oxygen atoms in 0.5 mol of SO_2
   b) hydrogen atoms in 2 mol of CH_4
   c) hydroxide ions in 0.1 mol of $Mg(OH)_2$
   d) ammonium ions in 1 mol of $(NH_4)_3PO_4$

2. Calculate the number of atoms in each of the following elements.
   a) 16 g of sulphur
   b) 100 g of calcium
   c) 0.001 g of carbon-14
   d) 8 g of oxygen

3. Calculate the number of molecules in each of the following compounds.
   a) 1.1 g of CO_2
   b) 200 g of H_2O
   c) 3.2 g of CH_4
   d) 5 g of $C_{12}H_{22}O_{11}$

4. Calculate the number of formula units in each of the following compounds.
   a) 10 g of $CaCO_3$
   b) 1.01 g of KNO_3
   c) 18.8 g of Li_2SO_4
   d) 1 kg of NaOH

5. Calculate the number of atoms in each of the following compounds.
   a) 1.8 g of H_2O
   b) 8.6 g of C_6H_{14}
   c) 3.4 g of NH_3
   d) 9.2 g of C_2H_5OH

6. Calculate the number of ions in each of the following compounds.
   a) 9.4 g of K_2O
   b) 14.8 g of $Ca(OH)_2$
   c) 585 g of NaCl
   d) 342 kg of $Al_2(SO_4)_3$

7. When potassium chlorate ($KClO_3$) is heated strongly, it decomposes to give potassium chloride and oxygen.
    Calculate the mass of potassium chlorate which would produce 1.8×10^{23} molecules of oxygen.

8. Calculate the number of molecules of hydrogen which are produced when excess magnesium reacts with 500 cm^3 of hydrochloric acid, concentration 1 mol l^{-1}.

9. Oxygen can be converted into its polymorph ozone, O_3, by electrical discharge, according to the equation:

    $$3O_2(g) \quad \rightarrow \quad 2O_3(g)$$

    If 4.8 g of oxygen gas is completely converted to ozone, how many molecules of ozone would be produced?

10. The isotope $^{131}_{53}I$ is radioactive and is manufactured for medicinal use by the neutron bombardment of the isotope $^{127}_{53}I$.

    $$^{127}_{53}I \quad + \quad 4^{1}_{0}n \quad \rightarrow \quad ^{131}_{53}I$$

    How many neutrons are required to produce 13.1 g of iodine-131?

Exercise 1.17   Molar volumes of gases

1.   The volume of 0.22 g of propene is 118 cm^3.
     Calculate the volume of 2 mol of propene.

2.   The volume of 1 g of hydrogen is 11.6 litres.
     Calculate the volume of 4 mol of hydrogen.

3.   A flask, capacity 600 cm^3, was used to calculate the molar volume of
     sulphur dioxide.
     The following data was obtained.
     Mass of evacuated flask   =   512.97 g
     Mass of flask + sulphur dioxide   =   514.57 g
     Calculate the molar volume of sulphur dioxide.

4.   From the data calculate the approximate formula mass of gas **X**.

         Mass of plastic bottle empty   =   112.80 g
         Mass of plastic bottle + gas **X**   =   113.52 g
         Capacity of plastic bottle   =   1 litre
         Molar volume of gas **X**   =   23.6 litres mol^{-1}

5.   Lithium hydroxide has been used to absorb carbon dioxide produced by
     astronauts.
              LiOH   +   CO$_2$ →   LiHCO$_3$
     6.0 g of lithium hydroxide absobs 5.9 litres of carbon dioxide.
     Calculate the molar volume of carbon dioxide.

In questions 6 to 9 of this exercise take the molar volume of the gases to be 23.0 litres mol^{-1}.

6. Calculate the volume of
    a) 10 g of neon,
    b) 3.2 g of oxygen.

7. Calculate the number of molecules in
    a) 2.3 litres of ammonia,
    b) 46 litres of hydrogen.

8. Phosphorus forms two hydrides, PH_3 and P_2H_4.
    0.152 g of a hydride of phosphorus has a volume of 100 cm^3.
    Calculate the mass of one mole of the hydride **and** identify it.

9. A weather balloon contains equal volumes of helium and hydrogen.
    If the total volume of the balloon is 9.2 litres, calculate the mass of each gas which will be present in the balloon.

In questions 10 and 11 use the densities of the gases given in your data booklet.

10. Calculate the volume of 10 g of
    a) hydrogen,
    b) argon.

11. Calculate the amount, in moles, of 10 litres of
    a) helium,
    b) nitrogen.

In question 12 of this exercise take the molar volume of the gases to be 23.2 litres mol^{-1}.

12. a) Calculate the volume of hydrogen gas produced when 13 g of zinc is added to excess dilute hydrochloric acid.

b) Calculate the volume of oxygen which is required to completely burn 4 g of sulphur.

c) Calculate the mass of water produced when 2 litres of hydrogen is burned in excess oxygen.

d) Hydrogen peroxide (H_2O_2) decomposes to give water and oxygen. Calculate the mass of hydrogen peroxide required to give 58 cm^3 of oxygen.

e) The first stage in the extraction of copper from sulphide ores such as chalcopyrite ($CuFeS_2$) involves heating the ore with sand and oxygen.

$$4CuFeS_2(s) \quad + \quad 2SiO_2(s) \quad + \quad 5O_2(g)$$
$$\rightarrow \quad 2Cu_2S.FeS(l) \quad + \quad 2FeSiO_3(l) \quad + \quad 4SO_2(g)$$

Calculate the volume of oxygen required to react completely with 1472 kg of chalcopyrite.

f) Hydrogen can be obtained by the reforming of hexane.

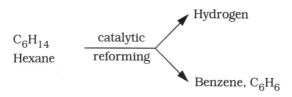

Calculate the volume of hydrogen which would be produced when 1 kg of hexane is reformed.

Exercise 1.18   Calculations involving volumes

In this exercise assume that all measurements are made at room temperature and atmospheric pressure, ie the same conditions of temperature and pressure.

1. In each of the following reactions calculate the ratio of the volume of product(s) to the volume of reactant(s).
    a) $H_2(g)$ + $Cl_2(g)$ → $2HCl(g)$
    b) $N_2(g)$ + $3H_2(g)$ → $2NH_3(g)$
    c) $2C(s)$ + $O_2(g)$ → $2CO(g)$
    d) $C_2H_4(g)$ + $3O_2(g)$ → $2CO_2(g)$ + $2H_2O(l)$
    e) $CuO(s)$ + $CO(g)$ → $Cu(s)$ + $CO_2(g)$

2. $N_2(g)$ + $2O_2(g)$ → $2NO_2(g)$

    Calculate the volume of nitrogen dioxide which is produced when 100 cm^3 of nitrogen is sparked in excess oxygen.

3. When each of the following volumes of gases is burned completely, calculate
    a) the volume of oxygen required,
    b) the volume of carbon dioxide produced.
        i) 100 cm^3 methane
        ii) 2 litres carbon monoxide
        iii) 250 cm^3 ethene
        iv) 150 cm^3 butane

4. $C_3H_8(g)$ + $5O_2(g)$ → $3CO_2(g)$ + $4H_2O(l)$

    10 cm^3 of propane gas is mixed with 75 cm^3 of oxygen and the mixture exploded.
    Calculate the volume and composition of the resulting gas mixture.

5. A mixture of 80 cm^3 of CO and 150 cm^3 of O$_2$ is exploded.
    a) Write a balanced equation for the reaction.
    b) After cooling, the residual gas is shaken with dilute sodium hydroxide solution.
        i) Which gas is absorbed by the sodium hydroxide solution?
        ii) What is the reduction in volume of the residual gas after shaking with the solution?
        iii) What volume of gas remains?

6. A gas mixture contains equal volumes of methane and hydrogen. Calculate the minimum volume of oxygen required for the complete combustion of 200 cm^3 of this mixture.

7. Xenon gas can react with fluorine gas to form xenon hexafluoride, XeF$_6$, which is a white solid at room temperature and atmospheric pressure.
    a) Write a balanced equation, with state symbols, for this reaction.
    b) Calculate the volume and composition of the gas remaining after 50 cm^3 of xenon and 400 cm^3 of fluorine react.

8. A mixture of 60 cm^3 of hydrogen and 40 cm^3 of carbon monoxide is passed over excess hot copper(II) oxide until no further reaction occurred.
    Calculate the volume and composition of the resulting gas mixture.

9. If 100 cm^3 of propene is burned completely with 900 cm^3 of oxygen, what will be the volume and composition of the resulting gas mixture?

10. 100 cm^3 of an unknown hydrocarbon gas, C$_X$H$_Y$, when completely burned, required 450 cm^3 of oxygen and produced 300 cm^3 of carbon dioxide.
    Calculate values for **X** and **Y**.

11. Gas syringes are graduated to allow the volume of gases to be measured. A heated box kept a syringe at a temperature greater than 100 °C. The syringe contained 150 cm^3 of hydrogen and 50 cm^3 of carbon monoxide mixed with 200 cm^3 of oxygen. When ignited the gases reacted as shown.

$$CO(g) \ + \ 3H_2(g) \ + \ 2O_2(g) \ \rightarrow \ CO_2(g) \ + \ 3H_2O(g)$$

a) Name the reactant gas which was in excess and give the remaining volume of this gas.

b) What was the volume and composition of the products of the reaction?

c) What would have been the reading on the gas syringe if, at the end of the reaction, the gases had been allowed to cool to room temperature?

12. A syringe was used to study the reactions of hydrocarbons with oxygen at a constant temperature of 120 °C.

In one experiment, 20 cm^3 of a hydrocarbon gas containing six carbon atoms per molecule was ignited in excess oxygen gas. Carbon dioxide and water were produced.

a) Calculate the volume of carbon dioxide produced.

b) 100 cm^3 of water vapour was produced.

What is the molecular formula of the hydrocarbon?

Unit 2　　The World of Carbon

Exercise 2.1　　　　　　　　　　　　　　　　　　　　Fuels

1.　To meet the specific requirement for high grade fuels, oil fractions have to be treated before use.

a)　What name is given to the industrial process in which reactions like the above occur.

b)　i)　Why were lead compounds added to some types of petrol?

　　ii)　Explain why the mixture of products is more suitable for use in unleaded petrol than is the reactant.

c)　Which of the products can be classified as aromatic?

2.　Hydrocarbons which are suitable for unleaded petrol are produced in oil refineries by a process called reforming.

a)　What is meant by reforming?

b)　Name the oil fraction which is used.

3.　Nitrogen oxides and carbon monoxide are polluting gases which are present in the exhaust mixtures from petrol engines.

a)　Explain the presence in car exhaust gases of

　　i)　nitrogen oxides,

　　ii)　carbon monoxide.

b)　In a catalytic converter, nitrogen oxides can react with carbon monoxide to form two non-toxic gases. Name these gases.

4. Petrols are blends of different hydrocarbons.
   a) What causes the mixture of petrol and air to ignite in a car engine?
   b) Why do winter blends of petrol in Scotland contain more hydrocarbons of low relative molecular mass?
   c) Why has the demand for blends with higher aromatic content increased in the last ten years?

5. Ethanol is being considered as an engine fuel in countries where it can be economically produced in sufficient quantities
   a) What is meant by a fuel?
   b) i) Name the process used to produce ethanol from sugar cane.
      ii) What is the main advantage of using this ethanol instead of petrol?

6. When farm manure and straw decay under anaerobic conditions a mixture known as biogas is produced.
   This consists of significant proportions of a fuel gas and carbon dioxide.
   a) What is meant by anaerobic conditions?
   b) Give another name for the process which occurs.
   c) Name the main component of the fuel gas.

7. Both hydrogen and methanol can be considered as alternative fuels to petrol.
   a) What is the main advantage of burning hydrogen compared with petrol.
   b) Give **one** advantage and **one** disadvantage of using methanol instead of petrol.

Exercise 2.2 Nomenclature and structural formulae - hydrocarbons

1. Give the systematic name for each of the following hydrocarbons.

a) $CH_3-CH-CH_2-CH_2-CH_3$
$\quad\quad\quad |$
$\quad\quad\quad CH_3$

b) $CH_3-CH-CH-CH_3$
$\quad\quad\quad |\quad\ |$
$\quad\quad\quad CH_3\ CH_3$

c) $\quad\quad\quad\quad\quad CH_3$
$\quad\quad\quad\quad\quad\ |$
$\quad CH_3-CH_2-CH$
$\quad\quad\quad\quad\quad\ |$
$\quad\quad\quad\quad\quad CH_2$
$\quad\quad\quad\quad\quad\ |$
$\quad\quad\quad\quad\quad CH_3$

d) $\quad\quad\quad CH_3$
$\quad\quad\quad\ |$
$\quad CH_3-C-CH_2-CH_3$
$\quad\quad\quad\ |$
$\quad\quad\quad CH_3$

e) $\quad\quad\quad\ CH_3$
$\quad\quad\quad\ \ |$
$\quad CH_3-C-CH=CH_2$
$\quad\quad\quad\ \ |$
$\quad\quad\quad\ CH_3$

f) $\quad\quad\ CH_3$
$\quad\quad\ \ |$
$\quad CH_3-CH-CH-CH_2-C\equiv CH$
$\quad\quad\quad\quad\ \ |$
$\quad\quad\quad\quad\ CH_2$
$\quad\quad\quad\quad\ \ |$
$\quad\quad\quad\quad\ CH_3$

g)
$CH_3-CH=CH-CH_2-CH-CH_3$
$\quad\quad\ |\quad\quad\quad\quad\quad |$
$\quad\quad CH_2\quad\quad\quad\ CH_3$
$\quad\quad\ |$
$\quad\quad CH_3$

h)
$CH_3-CH_2-C-CH_2-CH_3$
$\quad\quad\quad\quad ||$
$\quad\quad\quad\quad C$
$\quad\quad\quad\ /\quad \backslash$
$\quad\quad\quad H\quad\ H$

i) $CH_2-CH-CH_3$
$\quad |\quad\ \ |$
$\quad CH_2-CH_2$

j) $\quad\quad\quad CH_2$
$\quad\quad\ /\quad\quad \backslash$
$\quad CH_2\quad\quad CH-CH_3$
$\quad\ |\quad\quad\quad\ |$
$\quad CH_2\quad\quad CH-CH_3$
$\quad\quad \backslash\quad\quad /$
$\quad\quad\quad CH_2$

k) $\quad\quad\ CH_2$
$\quad\quad\ /\quad \backslash$
$\quad CH_2\quad\quad CH$
$\quad\ \backslash\quad\quad ||$
$\quad\ CH_2-C-CH_3$
$\quad\quad\ |$
$\quad\quad CH_3$

l)
$CH\equiv C-CH-CH_3$
$\quad\quad\quad |$
$\quad\quad\quad CH_3$

2. Draw the shortened structural formula and give the systematic name for each of the following hydrocarbons.

a) $CH_3CH_2C(CH_3)_2CH_2CH_3$

b) $CH_3CH(CH_3)CH(CH_3)CH(CH_3)_2$

c) $(CH_3)_4C$

d) $CH_2CHCH_2CH_3$

e) $CH_3CH_2CCCH_3$

f) $CH_3C(CH_3)_2CHCH_2$

g) $(CH_3)_2CCH_2$

h) $CHCC(CH_3)_2CH_2CH_3$

i) $(CH_3)_3CCCH$

3. Draw the shortened structural formula for each of the following hydrocarbons.

a) 3-ethylhexane

b) 2,2,4-trimethylpentane

c) 3-ethyl,2-methylpentane

d) pent-1-ene

e) 4,4-dimethyloct-1-yne

f) 2,3-dimethylbut-2-ene

g) 4-methylhex-2-yne

h) pent-1,3-diene

i) ethylcyclohexane

j). cyclopentene

k) 1,3-dimethylcyclopentane

4. Draw the shortened structural formula for each of the following hydrocarbons and give the systematic name.

a) the **three** straight-chain isomers of 1,2-dimethylcyclobutane

b) the **two** straight-chain isomers of cyclopentene

c) the **three** isomers of C_5H_{12}

d) the **five** isomers of C_4H_8

Exercise 2.3   Nomenclature and structural formulae
- alkanols

1. Give the systematic name for each of the following alkanols.

    a) CH_3-CH_2-OH

    b) $CH_3-CH-CH_2-CH_3$
        $\qquad\quad |$
        $\qquad\;\; OH$

    c)
    $$CH_3-CH_2-\overset{\overset{\displaystyle CH_3}{|}}{\underset{\underset{\displaystyle OH}{|}}{C}}-CH_3$$

    d)
    $$CH_3-\overset{}{\underset{\underset{\displaystyle OH}{|}}{CH}}-CH_2-\overset{\overset{\displaystyle CH_3}{|}}{CH}-CH_3$$

2. Draw the shortened structural formula for each of the following alkanols and give the systematic name.

    a) $CH_3CH_2CH_2OH$

    b) $CH_3CH(OH)CH_3$

    c) $CH_3CH_2C(CH_3)(OH)CH_2CH_3$

    d) $CH_3CH(OH)CH(CH_3)CH_3$

3. Draw the shortened structural formula for each of the following alkanols.

    a) butan-1-ol

    b) 2-methylhexan-3-ol

    c) 2,3-dimethylpentan-1-ol

    d) 3,3-dimethylbutan-2-ol

4. Ethan-1,2-diol is a dihydric alcohol used as anti-freeze for car cooling systems.

    a) Draw the full structural formula for ethan-1,2-diol.

    b) Suggest what is meant by a dihydric alcohol.

5. Two isomeric straight-chain alcohols, each having four carbon atoms, are known.

    a) Draw a structural formula for each of these alcohols.

    b) Draw a structural formula for the isomeric branched-chain alcohol.

Exercise 2.4   Nomenclature and structural formulae - alkanals, alkanones and alkanoic acids

1. Give the systematic name for each of the following carbonyl compounds.

   a) $CH_3-CH_2-\underset{\displaystyle H}{\overset{\displaystyle }{C}}{=}O$

   b) $CH_3-\underset{\displaystyle O}{\overset{\displaystyle }{C}}-CH_2-CH_2-CH_3$

   c) $CH_3-\underset{\displaystyle CH_3}{\overset{\displaystyle }{CH}}-CH_2-\underset{\displaystyle H}{\overset{\displaystyle }{C}}{=}O$

   d) $CH_3-\underset{\displaystyle O}{\overset{\displaystyle }{C}}-CH_2-\underset{\displaystyle CH_3}{\overset{\displaystyle CH_3}{C}}-CH_3$

2. Draw the shortened structural formula for each of the following carbonyl compounds and give the systematic name.

   a) CH_3CHO

   b) $CH_3CH_2COCH_3$

   c) $CH_3CH_2CH(CH_3)CHO$

   d) $CH_3C(CH_3)_2CH_2COCH_3$

3. Draw the shortened structural formula for each of the following carbonyl compounds.
   a) methanal
   b) propanone
   c) 3-ethylhexanal
   d) 3,3-dimethylhexan-2-one.

4. Give the systematic name for each of the following alkanoic acids.

   a) $H-\underset{\displaystyle }{\overset{\displaystyle O}{C}}-OH$

   b) $CH_3-\underset{\displaystyle CH_3}{\overset{\displaystyle }{CH}}-CH_2-\overset{\displaystyle O}{C}-OH$

   c) $CH_3-CH_2-\underset{\displaystyle CH_3}{\overset{\displaystyle }{CH}}-CH_2-\overset{\displaystyle O}{C}-OH$

5. Draw the shortened structural formula for each of the following alkanoic acids and give the systematic name.
   a) CH_3CH_2COOH
   b) $CH_3CH_2C(CH_3)_2CH_2COOH$
   c) $CH_3CH(CH_3)CH(CH_3)COOH$

6. Draw the shortened structural formula for each of the following acids.
   a) ethanoic acid
   b) 2-methylpentanoic acid
   c) 4,4-dimethylhexanoic acid

7. Compounds **A** and **B** are straight-chain isomers of pentan-2-one. Both also contain a carbonyl group.
   a) Draw structural formulae for compounds **A** and **B**.
   b) Name isomers **A** and **B**.

8. a) Draw a structural formula for butanoic acid.
   b) Draw a structural formula for an isomeric acid of butanoic acid.

9. a) Draw a structural formula for propanal.
   b) To which homologous series does propanal belong?
   c) i) Does propanal have an isomer which belongs to the same homologous series?
      ii) Explain your answer.
   d) Draw a structural formula for an isomer of propanal which is in a different homologous series.
   e) To which homologous series does this isomer belong?

10. When ozone, O_3, is bubbled into a solution of an alkene, an ozonide is formed. This compound decomposes on treatment with water.

(R and R' represent hydrogen atoms or alkyl groups.)

   a) To which homologous series do the substances **X** and **Y** belong?
   b) Give the systematic names of the products **X** and **Y** which would be formed if propene was used in the above reaction sequence.

Exercise 2.5   Nomenclature and structural formulae - esters

1. Name each of the following esters.

   a)
$$CH_3-\overset{\displaystyle O}{\overset{\|}{C}}-O-CH_3$$

   b)
$$CH_3-O-\overset{\displaystyle O}{\overset{\|}{C}}-H$$

   c) $CH_3COOCH_2CH_2CH_3$

   d) $HCOOCH_2CH_3$

2. Draw a structural formula for each of the following esters.
   a) ethyl ethanoate
   b) propyl butanoate

3. For each of the following parent alkanols and alkanoic acids, name the ester which is formed and draw a structural formula.
   a) ethanol / methanoic acid
   b) methanol / propanoic acid
   c) CH_3CH_2OH / CH_3COOH
   d) $CH_3CH_2CH_2OH / HCOOH$

4. For the breakdown of each of the following esters, name the products and draw their structural formulae.
   a) ethyl propanoate
   b) methyl ethanoate

   c)
$$CH_3CH_2-O-\overset{\displaystyle O}{\overset{\|}{C}}-H$$

   d)
$$CH_3CH_2CH_2-\overset{\displaystyle O}{\overset{\|}{C}}-O-CH_3$$

5. An organic compound has the formula $HCOOCH_3$.
   a) Name this compound.
   b) The compound can be broken up on treatment with sodium hydroxide solution.
      Name the **two** products of this reaction.

6. a) Draw structural formulae for the **two** esters which are isomers of propanoic acid.
   b) Name each of the esters.

Exercise 2.6   Nomenclature and structural formulae - aromatic compounds

1. a) Name the simplest member of the class of aromatic hydrocarbons.
    b) What is the formula for this hydrocarbon?
    c) Name the group with the formula -C_6H_5 found in aromatic hydrocarbons.

2. The benzene ring can be drawn in two ways.

    structure **A**   structure **B**

    Explain why structure **B** is considered to be a better representation of the benzene ring.

3. For the formula C_8H_{10}, there are **four** possible isomers which contain a benzene ring.

    Using the symbol ⬡ to represent the benzene ring, draw the structure of each isomer.

4. The structures of three useful aromatic products are shown.

    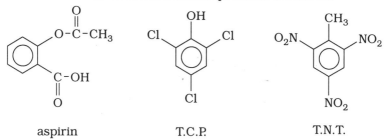

    aspirin   T.C.P.   T.N.T.

    Write the molecular formula for each.

5. Benzene molecules, like graphite, contain free (delocalised) electrons. Why then does benzene **not** conduct electricity?

Exercise 2.7   Cracking

1.   An example of cracking is shown in the equation.

$$C_8H_{18} \longrightarrow C_6H_{14} \quad + \quad \mathbf{X}$$

   a)   What is meant by cracking?
   b)   Draw a labelled diagram to show how the catalytic cracking can be
        carried out in a laboratory. Show how the gas **X** can be collected.
   c)   Find the formula and name of **X**.
   d)   Explain why cracking is one of the important processes carried out
        in an oil refinery.

2.   The cracking of paraffin can be carried out in the laboratory using strong
     heat. A mixture of saturated and unsaturated products is obtained.
   a)   What effect would a suitable catalyst have on the amount of heat
        needed to crack paraffin?
   b)   Explain why cracking produces a mixture of saturated and
        unsaturated products.

3.   Monomer **X**, which is used to make plastics, is obtained by the thermal
     cracking of 1,2-dichloroethane (EDC).

$$
\begin{array}{c}
\text{Cl} \ \ \text{Cl} \\
| \ \ \ | \\
\text{H-C-C-H} \\
| \ \ \ | \\
\text{H} \ \ \text{H}
\end{array}
\longrightarrow
\quad \text{monomer } \mathbf{X} \quad + \quad \text{hydrogen chloride}
$$

     During the cracking process side reactions, such as those below, can
     occur.

$$
\text{EDC} \longrightarrow
\begin{array}{c}
\text{Cl} \ \ \text{Cl} \\
| \ \ \ | \\
\text{C=C} \\
| \ \ \ | \\
\text{H} \ \ \text{H}
\end{array}
\quad + \quad \mathbf{Y}
$$

$$\text{or} \quad \text{EDC} \longrightarrow 2\mathbf{Z} \ + \ 2\text{HCl} \ + \ H_2$$

   a)   Name monomer **X**.
   b)   Name the "unwanted" products **Y** and **Z**.

Exercise 2.8 Addition reactions

1. New forms of pure carbon, called fullerenes, have been made recently. Fullerenes can be made into hydrocarbons. One such hydrocarbon has the formula $C_{60}H_{36}$.
   Describe a chemical test which could be carried out on a solution of $C_{60}H_{36}$ to show whether the hydrocarbon is saturated or unsaturated.

2. The following table gives information about the addition of bromine to four different hydrocarbons.

	Molecular formula of hydrocarbon	Addition compound formed on reaction with bromine
A	C_6H_{12}	$C_6H_{12}Br_2$
B	C_6H_{12}	No addition product formed
C	C_6H_{10}	$C_6H_{10}Br_4$
D	C_6H_{10}	$C_6H_{10}Br_2$

Draw a possible structural formula for the hydrocarbons **A**, **B**, **C** and **D**.

3. a) Draw the full structural formula for the product when each of the following hydrocarbons is bubbled through bromine solution.

   i)

   $$H-\underset{\underset{H}{|}}{\overset{\overset{H}{|}}{C}}-C=C-\underset{\underset{H}{|}}{\overset{\overset{H}{|}}{C}}-H$$

   ii)

   $$\underset{\underset{H}{|}}{\overset{\overset{H}{|}}{C}}=C-C=C-\underset{\underset{H}{|}}{\overset{\overset{H}{|}}{C}}-H$$

   b) Name each of the products.
   c) What name is given to the kind of reaction which takes place?

4.
$$\text{chloroethane} \xleftarrow{\text{H}_2} \textbf{X} \xrightarrow{\textbf{Y}} \text{1,2-dichloroethane}$$

a) Draw the full structural formula for compound **X**.

b) Name reagent **Y**.

5. In the commercial production of monochloroethene, the initial stage is the direct chlorination of ethene to form an intermediate compound known as EDC.

$$\text{ethene} \quad + \quad \text{chlorine} \quad \longrightarrow \quad \text{EDC}$$

The EDC is then purified and converted to monochloroethene and hydrogen chloride by a thermal cracking process.

At certain temperatures, monochloroethene recombines with hydrogen chloride to produce an isomer of EDC.

a) What type of chemical reaction is involved in the direct chlorination of ethene?

b) Draw a structural formula for
   i) monochloroethene,
   ii) the intermediate compound known as EDC,
   iii) the isomer of EDC produced by monochloroethene recombining with hydrogen chloride.

c) What is the systematic name for the compound known as EDC?

6. Compound **Q** reacts as follows.

$$C_6H_{11}Br \xleftarrow{} C_6H_{10} \xrightarrow[\text{heat, pressure}]{\text{H}_2 + \text{Ni catalyst}} C_6H_{12}$$

$$\textbf{P} \qquad\qquad\qquad \textbf{Q} \qquad\qquad\qquad \textbf{R}$$

a) Given that compound **R** does not readily undergo further addition, draw structural formulae for **P**, **Q** and **R**.

b) What reagent would be used to convert **Q** to **P**?

7. Ethyne can undergo addition reactions.

a) ethyne $\xrightarrow{\text{hydrogen}}$ **A** $\xrightarrow{\text{hydrogen}}$ **B**

    i) Name compound **A**,   ii) Name compound **B**.

b) ethyne $\xrightarrow{\text{chlorine}}$ **P** $\xrightarrow{\text{hydrogen chloride}}$ **Q**

    Draw a structural formula for
    i) compound **P**,
    ii) compound **Q**.

c) ethyne $\xrightarrow{\text{reagent } \textbf{X}}$ **Y** $\xrightarrow{\text{hydrogen}}$ $H-\overset{\displaystyle H}{\underset{\displaystyle H}{C}}-\overset{\displaystyle H}{\underset{\displaystyle H}{C}}-Cl$

    i) Name reagent **X**.
    ii) Draw a structural formula for compound **Y**.

8. Benzene has the formula C_6H_6.
a) Draw a structural formula for an isomer of benzene with
    i) an open chain structure,
    ii) a closed chain structure.
b) Describe **one** reaction which could be used to distinguish benzene from each of the above isomers.

9.
a) butan-2-ol $\xrightarrow[\text{heat}]{Al_2O_3}$ **A** + **B**

    i) Draw a structural formula for the isomeric hydrocarbons **A** and **B**.
    ii) Name the kind of reaction which takes place.
b) Isomers of pentanol can undergo a similar reaction.
    i) Name the **two** straight-chain isomers which form **one** product.
    ii) Name the straight-chain isomer which forms **two** products.

10. Ethanol can be prepared in industry by an addition reaction between steam and ethene.

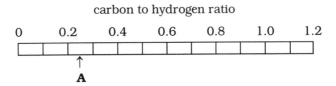

a) Give another name for this type of reaction.
b) Ethanol can be made by a reaction other than addition.
   Name this other type of reaction.

11. A ratio line can be used to illustrate the carbon to hydrogen ratio in different hydrocarbons.

carbon to hydrogen ratio

| 0 | 0.2 | 0.4 | 0.6 | 0.8 | 1.0 | 1.2 |

↑
A

Methane would appear at point **A**.

a) At what value would butane appear?
b) An unbranched hydrocarbon **X** with six carbon atoms per molecule has a carbon to hydrogen ratio of 0.5. **X** does not immediately decolourise bromine solution.
   Give a name for **X**.
c) One mole of a hydrocarbon **Y** with two carbon atoms per molecule reacts with two moles of bromine.
   At what value would **Y** appear?

Exercise 2.9   Primary, secondary and tertiary alcohols

1. State whether each of the following is a primary, secondary or a tertiary alcohol.

   a) $CH_3-CH_2-CH_2-OH$

   b)
   $$CH_3-\underset{\underset{OH}{|}}{\overset{\overset{CH_3}{|}}{C}}-CH_2-CH_3$$

   c)
   $$CH_3-\underset{\underset{OH}{|}}{CH}-\underset{\underset{CH_3}{|}}{\overset{\overset{CH_3}{|}}{C}}-CH_3$$

   d)
   $$HO-CH_2-\underset{}{\overset{\overset{CH_3}{|}}{CH}}-CH_2-CH_3$$

   e) CH_3-CH_2-OH

   f)
   $$CH_3-\underset{\underset{CH_3}{|}}{\overset{\overset{CH_3}{|}}{C}}-\underset{\underset{OH}{|}}{CH}-CH_3$$

2. State whether each of the following is a primary, secondary or tertiary alcohol.
   a) butan-2-ol
   b) pentan-1-ol
   c) 2-methylbutan-1-ol
   d) 3,3-dimethylpentan-2-ol
   e) 3-ethylpentan-3-ol
   f) 2,3,3-trimethylhexan-2-ol.

3. Copy the following carbon skeleton three times and add one hydroxyl group to each to make a primary, secondary and tertiary alcohol.

$$\begin{array}{c} -\overset{|}{\underset{|}{C}}- \\ -\overset{|}{\underset{|}{C}}-\overset{|}{\underset{|}{C}}-\overset{|}{\underset{|}{C}}-\overset{|}{\underset{|}{C}}- \end{array}$$

Exercise 2.10   Oxidation

1. $$\text{alcohol } \mathbf{X} \xrightarrow{\ \mathbf{Z}\ } \text{compound } \mathbf{Y} \longrightarrow CH_3-\overset{\displaystyle O}{\overset{\|}{C}}-OH$$

   a)   Name alcohol **X**.
   b)   Draw a structural formula for compound **Y**.
   c)   Name a reagent which could be used at **Z**.

2.   Draw a structural formula for the carbonyl compound which
   a)   can be oxidised to ethanoic acid,
   b)   can be oxidised to 2-methylpropanoic acid,
   c)   is formed by the oxidation of propan-2-ol,
   d)   is formed by the oxidation of 2-methylbutan-1-ol.

3.   Primary alcohols may be oxidised to carboxylic acids in two stages.
   a)   Draw the full structural formula for each product obtained by the
        oxidation of the following compound.

$$\begin{array}{c} \quad\;\, H\;\; H\;\; H \\ \quad\;\, |\quad |\quad | \\ H-C-C-C-OH \\ \quad\;\, |\quad |\quad | \\ \quad\;\, H\;\; H\;\; H \end{array}$$

   b)   Name each of the products.
   c)   What colour change is observed when the compound is oxidised by
        acidified potassium dichromate solution?

4.   An alcohol **X**, on mild oxidation, gives a compound **Y**, of molecular mass
     72. Compound **Y** can **not** be oxidised further.
   a)   Draw structural formulae for **X** and **Y**.
   b)   Give the systematic name for alcohol **X**.
   c)   Is **X** a primary, secondary or tertiary alcohol?

5.   An aldehyde can be prepared by oxidation of the corresponding alcohol.
   a)   Name the alcohol you would use to prepare butanal.
   b)   One test for aldehydes is the Benedict's test, in which copper(II) ions
        are reduced.
        To what compound would propanal be converted during this test?
   c)   What colour change is observed when propanal is oxidised by
        Benedict's solution?

6.

$$C_6H_{12}O \xrightarrow{\text{oxidation}} \text{cyclohexanone}$$

compound **A**

a)   Draw a structural formula for cyclohexanone.

b)   Name the compound **A**.

7.   Butanone is an important industrial solvent. It is formed by the catalytic dehydrogenation of butan-2-ol for which the word equation is:

$$\text{butan-2-ol} \xrightarrow[\text{catalyst}]{\text{zinc oxide}} \text{butanone} + \text{hydrogen}$$

a)   Draw a structural formula for
      i)   butan-2-ol,
      ii) butanone.

b)   Give another name for the process described as "dehydrogenation".

c)   Why does catalytic dehydrogenation not occur if the butan-2-ol is replaced by 2-methylpropan-2-ol?

8.   Acrolein is a feedstock for the production of useful organic compounds, eg acrylic fibres, synthetic rubber and glycerol.
     Acrolein can take part in both oxidation and reduction reactions.

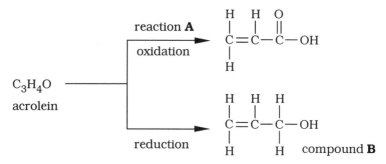

a)   Draw a structural formula for acrolein.

b)   Why can reaction **A** be classified as oxidation?

c)   Compound **B** has an isomer which belongs to a different homologous series and has no effect on Benedict's solution.
     Draw a structural formula for this isomer.

Exercise 2.11   Making and breaking esters

1.

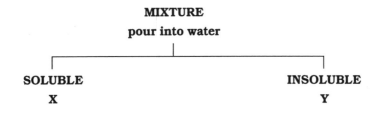

$$CH_3-\overset{\displaystyle O}{\overset{\|}{C}}-O-\underset{\displaystyle CH_3}{\overset{\displaystyle |}{CH}}-C_2H_5$$

   a)   Give the systematic names of the **two** compounds which, when
        warmed with concentrated sulphuric acid, react to form the above
        ester.

   b)   Unless the ester is removed from the reaction mixture as it forms,
        100% conversion of reactants to ester is never achieved.
        Give the reason for this.

2.   Preparation of ethyl ethanoate from ethanoic acid and ethanol results in
     an equilibrium mixture.

$$CH_3COOH \; + \; C_2H_5OH \; \rightleftharpoons \; CH_3COOC_2H_5 \; + \; H_2O$$

MIXTURE

pour into water

SOLUBLE	INSOLUBLE
X	**Y**

   a)   Name the kind of reaction which takes place in the preparation.
   b)   Name the substances present at **X** and **Y**.

4. a) Salicylic acid occurs in the form of its methyl ester as a constituent of oil of wintergreen, in the North American health plant, Gaultheria Procumbens. The formula for salicylic acid may be represented:

COOH

OH

Draw a structural formula for the ester formed when salicylic acid reacts with methanol.

b) Acetylsalicylic acid is widely used as a pain killer under its commercial name "Aspirin". The formula may be written as:

COOH

$$O-\overset{\overset{\displaystyle O}{\|}}{C}-CH_3$$

i) What is meant by hydrolysis?

ii) Draw structural formulae for the products of the hydrolysis of Aspirin.

iii) Suggest why Aspirin tablets which are kept for many months, especially in hot and humid climates, often smell of vinegar (ethanoic acid).

5. The artificial sweetener, aspartame, is a dimethyl ester of the dipeptide shown.

$$HO-\overset{\overset{\displaystyle CH_2}{|}}{\underset{\underset{\displaystyle O}{\|}}{C}}-CH-NH-\overset{\overset{\displaystyle O}{\|}}{C}-\overset{\overset{\displaystyle NH_2}{|}}{CH}-CH_2-\overset{\overset{\displaystyle O}{\|}}{C}-OH$$

Draw a structural formula for aspartame.

Exercise 2.12   Percentage yields

1. CH_3OH + C_2H_5COOH $\rightleftharpoons$ $C_2H_5COOCH_3$ + H_2O
         methanol   methyl propanoate

   In a preparation, 40.4 g of methyl propanoate is obtained from 18.3 g of methanol.
   Calculate the percentage yield.

2. C_3H_7OH $\longrightarrow$ C_2H_5CHO
           propan-1-ol   propanal

   In a preparation, 3.2 g of propanal is obtained from 3.9 g of propan-1-ol.
   Calculate the percentage yield.

3.

```
 H   H                        H H H
 |   |                        | | |
 C=C-C-H   +   Br₂   ⟶    H-C-C-C-H
 | | |                        | | |
 H H H                        Br Br H
```

   In a preparation, 20.4 g of 1,2-dibromopropane is obtained from 5.2 g of propene.
   Calculate the percentage yield.

4. $N_2(g)$ + $3H_2(g)$ $\rightleftharpoons$ $2NH_3(g)$

   Under test conditions, 2 kg of hydrogen reacts with excess nitrogen to produce 10 kg of ammonia.
   Calculate the percentage yield.

5. $2SO_2(g)$ + $O_2(g)$ $\rightleftharpoons$ $2SO_3(g)$

   Under test conditions, 1 tonne of sulphur dioxide reacts with excess oxygen to produce 0.8 tonnes of sulphur trioxide.
   Calculate the percentage yield.
   (1 tonne = 1000 kg)

Exercise 2.13   Uses of carbon compounds

1. There are competing demands for the use of crude oil. Give **three** examples of
    a) fuels based on petroleum compounds,
    b) types of petroleum-based consumer products.

2. Carbon compounds have a variety of uses. Give **two** uses for
    a) esters,   b) carboxylic acids.

3. Ozone is produced in the Earth's upper atmosphere by reactions involving molecules and atoms.
    a) i)   Write the formula for ozone.
        ii) Why is ozone thought to be such an important gas in the upper layers of the atmosphere?
    b) The depletion of the ozone layer has recently become a matter of concern.
        i)   What is thought to be causing the depletion?
        ii) Give **two** examples of possible consequences of depletion.

4. Chlorofluorocarbons, commonly known as CFCs, have useful properties.
    a) Give **three** uses for CFCs.
    b) Information about three CFCs is given in the table.

CFC	Name	Structure
12	dichlorodifluoromethane	...
13	1,1,2-trichloro-1,2,2-trifluoroethane	F—C—C—Cl with F, Cl above and Cl, F below
114	...	Cl—C—C—Cl with F, F above and F, F below

       i)   Draw the full structural formula for CFC 12.
       ii) Give the name for CFC 114.

Exercise 2.14   Early plastics and fibres (i)

1. Ethene can be formed by cracking the ethane from natural gas.
   a) Name the hydrocarbon in natural gas which can be cracked to form propene.
   b) Write a balanced equation for this reaction.
   c) Ethene and propene can also be formed by cracking a fraction from oil. Name this fraction.

2. Poly(propene) is used to make many kitchen items.
   a) Name the monomer unit from which poly(propene) is made.
   b) Draw a structural formula for the monomer unit.
   c) Draw the structure of part of a poly(propene) chain to show how **three** monomer units have joined together.

3. Polyvinyl chloride (PVC) is a well known polymer.

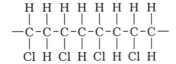

   a) How many repeating units are shown?
   b) Draw the full structural formula for the monomer unit.
   c) What type of polymerisation occurs in the formation of this polymer?

4. PTFE is an addition polymer made from tetrafluoroethene.
   a) What does PTFE stand for?
   b) Draw the full structural formula for tetrafluoroethene.
   c) Draw the structure of part of a PTFE chain to show how **three** monomer units have joined together.

5. The diagram shows part of the structure of a molecule of Orlon.

$$-CH_2-CH-CH_2-CH-CH_2-CH-$$
$$CNCNCN$$

a) Draw the structure of the repeating unit of Orlon.
b) Draw a structural formula for the monomer used to make Orlon.
c) State whether Orlon is made by addition or condensation polymerisation.

6.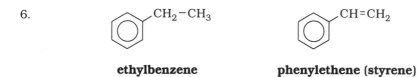

    ethylbenzene   **phenylethene (styrene)**

a) Describe a test which could be used to distinguish ethylbenzene from styrene.
b) Which of the above molecules would undergo polymerisation?
c) What type of polymerisation would occur?
d) Draw the structure of part of the polymer chain to show how **three** monomer units have joined together.

7. Perspex is as transparent as glass but does not break easily. This polymer is therefore used to make safety screens, spectacle lenses, and aeroplane windows.
    The following diagram shows part of a molecule of perspex.

$$
\begin{array}{ccccccccc}
H & & CH_3 & H & & CH_3 & H & & CH_3 & H & & CH_3 \\
| & & | & | & & | & | & & | & | & & | \\
-C & - & C & - & C & - & C & - & C & - & C & - & C & - & C & - \\
| & & | & | & & | & | & & | & | & & | \\
COOCH_3 & H & & COOCH_3 & H & & COOCH_3 & H & & COOCH_3 & H
\end{array}
$$

a) Draw the structure of the repeating unit in perspex.
b) Draw a structural formula for the monomer used to make perspex.
c) What type of polymerisation takes place when perspex is formed from the monomer?

8. Poly(butene) is used to make pipes which carry hot water under pressure. This is very useful in plumbing and underfloor heating. Poly(butene) is made using but-1-ene monomer.

```
     H H H H
     | | | |
     C=C-C-C-H
     |   | |
     H   H H
```

a) Draw the structure of part of the poly(butene) chain which is formed by **three** monomer units linking together.

b) Name the kind of polymerisation which takes place.

c) But-1-ene has a number of isomers. Draw a strucural formula for an isomer which
   i) could be used to form a polymer,
   ii) could **not** be used to form a polymer.

9. Part of the structure of a polymer molecule is shown.

```
  H Cl H H H Cl H H H Cl H H
  | |  | | | |  | | | |  | |
 —C-C=C-C-C-C=C-C-C-C=C-C—
  |    | |    | |    |
  H    H H    H H    H
```

a) Draw the structure of the repeating unit.

b) Describe a chemical test which could be used to distinguish between this polymer and poly(ethene).

10. Bucrylate is an ester which is used in surgery for repairing torn tissue.

```
      H    CN
      |    |
  H—C=C—C—O—CH₂—CH—CH₃
           ‖          |
           O          CH₃
```

It instantaneously polymerises when it comes into contact with ionic solutions.

a) What type of polymerisation will bucrylate undergo?

b) Draw the structure of the repeating unit in polybucrylate.

Exercise 2.15   Early plastics and fibres (ii)

1. The flow diagram shows how a polyamide, used in the preparation of polyurethane foam, is manufactured.

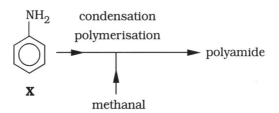

a) Draw the full structural formula for methanal.
b) Draw a possible structure for the compound formed when **two** molecules of compound **X** and **one** molecule of methanal react by a condensation reaction.

2. The simplified flow diagram shows how methanal can be manufactured from methane.

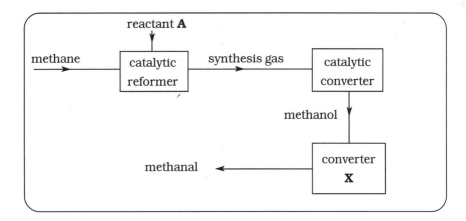

a) Name a source of methane.
b) Name reactant **A**.
c) Name the **two** gases which make up synthesis gas.
d) What kind of reaction takes place in converter **X**?
e) State an industrial use for methanal.

3. The flow chart presents some information about feedstocks from coal.

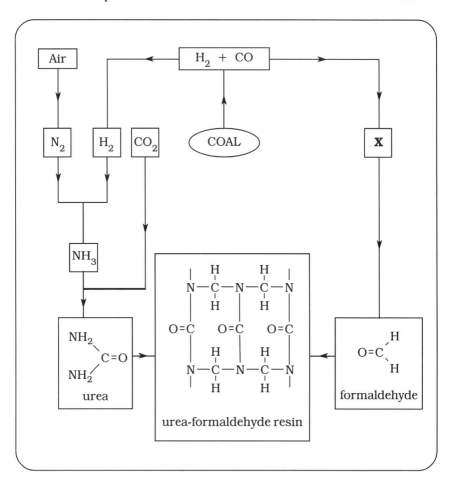

a) What is the industrial name for the mixture of carbon monoxide and hydrogen produced from coal?

b) Formaldehyde is formed by the oxidation of compound **X**.
    Draw the full structural formula for compound **X**.

c) What is the systematic name for formaldehyde?

d) By referring to the structure of the urea-formaldehyde resin, explain why it is a thermosetting polymer.

4. Polymerisation occurs between the following two compounds.

$$H_2NCH_2CH_2NH_2$$

A

$$HO-\overset{\overset{\textstyle O}{\|}}{C}-\!\!\left\langle\bigcirc\right\rangle\!\!-\overset{\overset{\textstyle O}{\|}}{C}-OH$$

B

a) To which classes of organic compounds do **A** and **B** belong?

b) Which type of polymerisation occurs between these two compounds?

c) Draw the structure of part of the polymer chain showing **two** of each monomer unit linked together.

5. Terylene is a synthetic condensation polymer. It is made from the two monomers shown .

A   is

$$HO-\overset{\overset{\textstyle H}{|}}{\underset{\underset{\textstyle H}{|}}{C}}-\overset{\overset{\textstyle H}{|}}{\underset{\underset{\textstyle H}{|}}{C}}-OH$$

B   is

$$HO-\overset{\overset{\textstyle O}{\|}}{C}\qquad\overset{\overset{\textstyle O}{\|}}{C}-OH$$
$$\bigcirc$$

These monomer units join in the order:

a) Name the small molecule which is usually a product in a condensation reaction.

b) Draw the structure of part of the polymer showing how **two** of each of the monomer units have joined together.

c) Name **one** other synthetic condensation polymer.

6. Caprolactam is an intermediate in the manufacture of nylon. The structure of caprolactam is:

a) i) In a polymeriser, water in catalytic amounts reacts with a small percentage of the caprolactam, opening the ring by hydrolysis and producing a molecule with two different functional groups.
   Draw a structural formula for the molecule produced.

   ii) This molecule initiates a chain reaction with other caprolactam molecules. As a result, each ring is opened and the molecules join head to tail, to form a long chain molecule (nylon 6) which has the structure:

$$-N-(CH_2)_5-C-N-(CH_2)_5-C-N-(CH_2)_5-C-$$

with H on the N atoms and O on the C atoms:

$$\begin{array}{cccc} -N-(CH_2)_5-\underset{\parallel}{C}-N-(CH_2)_5-\underset{\parallel}{C}-N-(CH_2)_5-\underset{\parallel}{C}- \\ H \qquad\quad O\;\;H \qquad\quad O\;\;H \qquad\quad O \end{array}$$

   Draw the structure of the repeating unit of nylon 6.

b) The structure of nylon 6,6 is:

$$\begin{array}{ccccc} -N-(CH_2)_6-N-C-(CH_2)_4-C-N-(CH_2)_6-N-C-(CH_2)_4-C- \\ H \qquad H\;\;O \qquad\quad O\;\;H \qquad\quad H\;\;O \qquad\quad O \end{array}$$

   i) Draw the structure of the repeating unit of nylon 6,6.

   ii) Draw structural formulae for the **two** monomers from which nylon 6,6 is made.

   iii) What type of condensation polymer is nylon 6,6?

c) Nylon is a very important engineering plastic.
   Explain why nylon is so strong.

7. The diagram shows part of the structure of a molecule of Terylene.

$$-\overset{\overset{\displaystyle O}{\|}}{C}-\!\!\!\bigcirc\!\!\!-\overset{\overset{\displaystyle O}{\|}}{C}-O-CH_2-CH_2-O-\overset{\overset{\displaystyle O}{\|}}{C}-\!\!\!\bigcirc\!\!\!-\overset{\overset{\displaystyle O}{\|}}{C}-O-CH_2-CH_2-O-$$

a) Draw the structure of the repeating unit.

b) Draw a structural formula for each of the monomers used to make Terylene.

c) What type of polymer is Terylene?

8. Some polymeric esters (polyesters) have a linear structure; others have a three-dimensional structure.

a) Give a use for each type of polymeric ester.

b) i) Draw a diagram to show the structure of **two** repeating units in the polyester which would be formed from the following monomers.

$$HO-\overset{\overset{\displaystyle O}{\|}}{C}-(CH_2)_4-\overset{\overset{\displaystyle O}{\|}}{C}-OH \qquad HO-(CH_2)_2-OH$$

ii) What kind of reaction would take place?

iii) Explain why the reaction would not produce a polymeric ester with a three-dimensional structure.

9. BIOPOL-PHBV is a recently launched biodegradable polyester.

$$-O-\overset{\overset{\displaystyle CH_3}{|}}{CH}-CH_2-\overset{\overset{\displaystyle O}{\|}}{C}-O-\overset{\overset{\displaystyle C_2H_5}{|}}{CH}-CH_2-\overset{\overset{\displaystyle O}{\|}}{C}-O-\overset{\overset{\displaystyle CH_3}{|}}{CH}-CH_2-\overset{\overset{\displaystyle O}{\|}}{C}-$$

a) Suggest why BIOPOL-PHBV can be used for polyester fibres but **not** polyester resins.

b) The first step in the biodegradation of BIOPOL-PHBV involves hydrolysis of the ester linkages giving **two** similar compounds. Draw a structural formula for each of these compounds.

1. Kevlar is a polymer which, weight for weight, is five times as strong as steel. Part of the molecular structure is shown.

a) Kevlar is a condensation polymer.
    Give **two** other terms which can be used to describe the structure of Kevlar.
b) Explain why Kevlar is strong.
c) Give **two** uses for Kevlar.

2. Part of a polymer structure is shown.

a) Name the polymer.
b) Draw the full structural formula for the monomer from which it is made.
c) This polymer can be treated to make a polymer which conducts electricity.
    i) Why does it conduct electricity?
    ii) Give **one** use for the polymer.

3. Polyvinyl carbazole is an unusual polymer.
    a) What unusual property does it have?
    b) Give **one** use for the polymer.

4. Poly(ethenol) is a recently developed plastic which is soluble in water. It is made by the reactions shown.

a) Name the type of reaction taking place
   i) at Step 1,
   ii) at Step 2.
b) Give **one** use for poly(ethenol).
c) Explain why poly(ethenol) is soluble in water.

5. a) State what is meant by
      i) a biodegradable polymer,
      ii) a photodegradable polymer.
   b) Give **one** example of each kind of polymer.
   c) Why is each a useful property?

Exercise 2.17   Fats and oils

1. a) Give **one** reason why fats and oils can be a useful part of a balanced
        diet.
    b) Explain why oils tend to have lower melting points than fats.

2. The structure of an oil can be represented as shown.

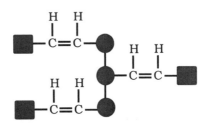

    a) Draw the structure of the fat which could be produced by "hardening"
        this oil.
    b) What is the effect of hardening on the melting point of this oil?
    c) Name the kind of chemical reaction which takes place during the
        hardening process.

3. The hydrolysis of fats produces fatty acids and glycerol.
    a) Draw a structural formula for glycerol.
    b) State the ratio of glycerol molecules to fatty acid molecules.

4. A triglyceride produces only glycerol and palmitic acid,
    $CH_3(CH_2)_{14}COOH$, on hydrolysis.
    a) To which set of compounds do triglycerides belong?
    b) Draw a structural formula for the triglyceride.
    c) Explain whether the triglyceride is likely to be a fat or an oil.

5. Mutton fat contains a compound called tristearin.

$$
\begin{array}{c}
\text{H} \quad\ \ \text{O} \\
| \qquad \| \\
\text{H-C-O-C-C}_{17}\text{H}_{35} \\
| \qquad \text{O} \\
\quad\ \ \| \\
\text{H-C-O-C-C}_{17}\text{H}_{35} \\
| \qquad \text{O} \\
\quad\ \ \| \\
\text{H-C-O-C-C}_{17}\text{H}_{35} \\
| \\
\text{H}
\end{array}
$$

Tristearin is broken down in the body during digestion.
a) Name the kind of chemical reaction which takes place.
b) The break down of tristearin produces a fatty acid.
   i) Is the fatty acid saturated or unsaturated?
   ii) Name the other product of this reaction.

6. Soaps can be produced by the reaction of fats and oils with sodium hydroxide solution.
   a) Name the kind of reaction which takes place.
   b) Describe the structure of a soap.

Exercise 2.18 Proteins

1. a) Give **one** reason why proteins are an essential part of a balanced diet.
    b) What kind of molecules are formed by the hydrolysis of proteins?
    c) Name **four** elements found in all proteins.

2. Glycine is an amino acid with the following structure.

$$\begin{array}{ccc} H & & O \\ | & & || \\ H-N-CH_2-C-OH \end{array}$$

    a) Draw the structure of **three** repeating units in the polymer which would be formed from glycine.
    b) What kind of reaction would be taking place?
    c) The body cannot make all the amino acids required for proteins and is dependent on dietary protein for the supply of certain amino acids.
        What name is given to such amino acids?

3. The diagram shows how amino acids are linked together in a protein.

$$\begin{array}{c} CH_3 \qquad\qquad\qquad CH_3 \\ | \qquad\qquad\qquad\qquad | \\ -N-CH_2-C-N-C-C-N-CH_2-C-N-C-C- \\ | \quad\quad || \ | \ | \quad || \ | \qquad || \ | \ | \quad || \\ H \qquad O\ H\ H\ \ O\ H \qquad O\ H\ H\ \ O \end{array}$$

    a) Draw the structure of the part of the molecule known as the peptide link.
    b) i)   How many different amino acids would be produced in the breakdown of this part of the polymer?
        ii) Draw a structural formula for each of these amino acids.
        iii) What kind of reaction would be taking place?

4. Enzymes are responsible for catalysing most of the reactions which take place in a cell, eg the hydrolysis of fats, sugars and proteins.
   a) To which set of compounds do enzymes belong?
   b) Use diagrams to describe how an enzyme could catalyse a specific reaction occurring in a cell.

5. The artificial sweetener, aspartame, has the strucure shown.

Aspartame's sweetness depends on the shape and structure of the molecule. **Two** amino acids, aspartic acid and phenylalanine, are formed when it is hydrolysed.
   a) Draw a structural formula for each of the amino acids produced during hydrolysis.
   b) Suggest a reason why aspartame is **not** used in food that will be cooked, but can be used in cold drinks.

6. Maltase is an enzyme which has optimum activity in alkaline conditions.
   a) Why does maltase catalyse the hydrolysis of maltose but **not** the hydrolysis of sucrose?
   b) Why does maltase lose its ability to act as a catalyst in acid conditions?
   c) State **one** other factor which can affect the efficiency of an enzyme.

Exercise 2.19   Miscellaneous

1. The flow diagram shows three steps in the preparation of a plastic from propane feedstock.

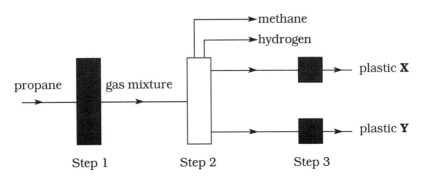

a) Name the process which occurs in Step 1.
b) Name the process which occurs in Step 2.
c) Name the process which occurs in Step 3.

2.

$$CH_3CH_2OH \xrightarrow{\text{heated aluminium oxide}} A$$

$$\begin{matrix} CH_3CH_2 \\ \diagdown \\ CHOH \\ \diagup \\ CH_3CH_2 \end{matrix} \xrightarrow{\text{acidified dichromate solution}} B$$

$$CH_3CH_2CHO \xrightarrow{\text{Benedict's solution}} C$$

Draw a structural formulae for the products **A**, **B** and **C**.

3.

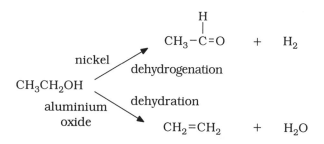

a) Draw a diagram of the apparatus which could be used to find out which of the two organic products above, results when ethanol is passed over hot zinc oxide.

b) Describe how to establish which product is formed.

4. 3-methylbut-1-ene reacts with concentrated sulphuric acid and the product obtained is hydrolysed with water to produce alcohol **A**.

$$CH_3CH(CH_3)CH(OH)CH_3$$

alcohol **A**

a) Draw a structural formula for 3-methylbut-1-ene.

b) Which class of organic compound is formed on mild oxidation of alcohol **A**?

c) Alcohol **A** reacts further with reagent **B** to produce two isomeric alkenes.

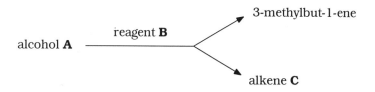

i) Name reagent **B**.

ii) Draw a structural formula for alkene **C**.

d) Draw a structural formula for the compound formed when 3-methylbut-1-ene reacts with chlorine.

5.

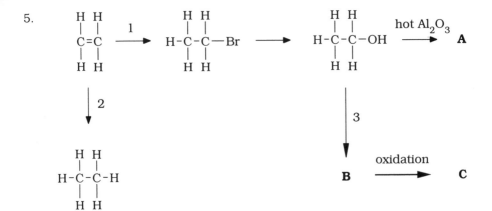

a) Draw the full structural formulae for compounds **A**, **B** and **C**.
b) Name the reagents at 1, 2 and 3.

6. An unknown liquid, formula C_3H_6O, is involved in the tests shown.

Test	Reagent	Observation
A	Bromine water	No reaction
B	2,4 DNP (test for carbonyl group)	orange precipitate (positive result)
C	Benedict's solution	No reaction

a) State what can be deduced about the structure of the liquid from
   i) test **A**,
   ii) tests **B** and **C** together.
b) Name the liquid and draw its full structural formula.

7. Propanone is a widely used solvent. It can be made from propene. Using structural formulae show the steps involved in this preparation and name the reagents used in each step.

8.

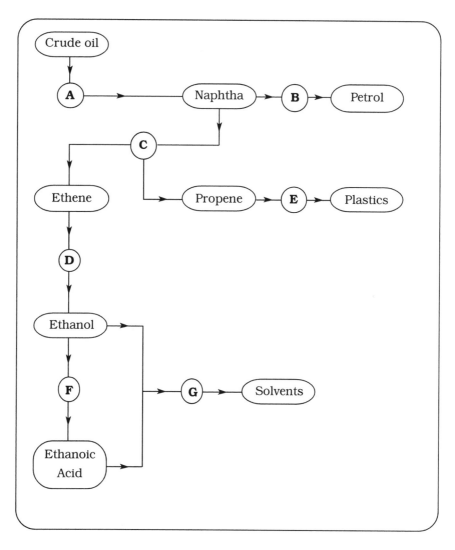

The simplified flow chart shows some of the processes used in the production of petroleum based consumer goods.

Processes **A** to **G** are contained in the following list.

> addition polymerisation, catalytic hydration, condensation, condensation polymerisation, cracking, fermentation, fractional distillation, oxidation, reforming.

Identify the processes **A** to **G**.

9.

$$C_3H_6 \xrightarrow{\ 1\ } C_3H_7Br \longrightarrow C_3H_7OH \xrightarrow{\ 2\ } C_3H_6O$$

$$\mathbf{A} \qquad\qquad \mathbf{B} \qquad\qquad \mathbf{C} \qquad\qquad \mathbf{D}$$

The above reaction scheme outlines the conversion of an alkene **A** to a ketone **D**.

a) Draw full structural formulae for **A**, **C** and **D**.

b) Name the type of reaction which takes place at 1 and 2 respectively.

10. Butan-1-ol can be converted into other compounds.

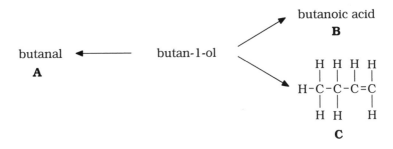

butanoic acid
B

butanal ⟵——— butan-1-ol
A

C

a) Draw a structural formula for
    i)   an isomer of **A** which belongs to the **same** homologous series as **A**,
    ii) an isomer of **A** which belongs to a **different** homologous series from **A**.

b) Which **two** compounds in the above flow chart can be formed from butan-1-ol by the same type of chemical reaction?

c) Describe a test which could be used to distinguish between **A** and **C**.

d) Name the reagent which could be used to convert butan-1-ol to
    i)   **A**,
    ii) **C**.

e) Compound **C** undergoes addition polymerisation.
    i)   Name the polymer formed.
    ii) Draw the structure of part of the polymer showing **three** monomer units linked together.

11.

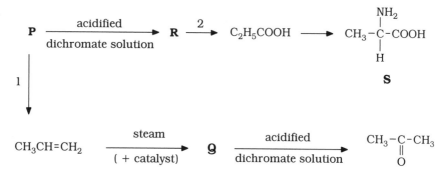

The reaction scheme shows a number of common reactions.

a)   Name compounds **P** and **Q**.
b)   State the types of chemical reaction occurring at 1 and 2.
c)   Draw a structural formula for compound **R**.
d)   Name the **two** functional groups in compound **S**.

12.

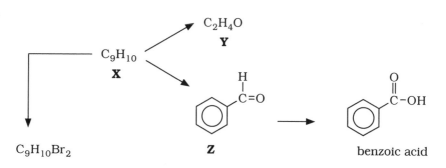

a)   From its reaction with bromine, which functional group must compound **X** contain?
b)   Draw a structural formula for compound **X**.
c)   Give **two** terms which can be used to describe the organic compound **Z**.
d)   Name a reagent capable of converting compound **Z** to benzoic acid.
e)   Compound **Y** is a member of the same homologous series as compound **Z**.
     Draw the full structural formula for compound **Y**.

13. There are four isomeric alcohols of molecular formula C_4H_9OH. Their structural formulae are as follows.

$$CH_3-CH_2-CH_2-CH_2-OH$$

(I)

$$CH_3-CH_2-\underset{\underset{OH}{|}}{CH}-CH_3$$

(II)

$$CH_3-\underset{\underset{CH_3}{|}}{\overset{\overset{CH_3}{|}}{C}}-OH$$

(III)

$$CH_3-\underset{\underset{CH_3}{|}}{CH}-CH_2-OH$$

(IV)

a) i) Give systematic names for compounds (I), (II), (III) and (IV).

ii) State which of the compounds (I) to (IV) are primary, which secondary and which tertiary alcohols.

b) The four alcohols are contained separately in four bottles marked **A**, **B**, **C** and **D**.
From the following information decide which bottle contains which alcohol.
State your reason briefly at each stage.

i) The contents of **A**, **B** and **C** can be readily oxidised by acidified potassium dichromate solution, while those of **D** cannot.

ii) **A** and **B** on complete oxidation by acidified dichromate solution give acids of formulae C_3H_7COOH; **C** does not give this acid.

iii) All four substances can be dehydrated to give alkenes. **A** and **D** can both form the same alkene. **B** and **C** can both form the same alkene, which is an isomer of that formed by **A** and **D**.

14. A gaseous compound **X** is known to be an alkene with a molecular formula of C_4H_8.

a) Draw structural formulae for **two** straight-chain alkenes and **one** branched-chain alkene having this molecular formula.

b) The position of the double bond in an alkene may be determined by a process called ozonolysis, in which the alkene is split (by ozone) at the double bond to give two carbonyl compounds.

| alkene | alkanals and/or alkanones |

R_1, R_2, R_3 and R_4 are hydrogen atoms or alkyl groups.
When the numbers and arrangements of carbon atoms in the products are known, the position of the double bond in the original alkene, and hence its structure, may be determined.
On ozonolysis, alkene **X** formed two compounds **Y** and **Z**. Only **Y** gave a positive test with Benedict's solution.

i) What would be seen to indicate a positive result in the Benedict's test?

ii) What do the actual test results indicate about the structures of carbonyl compounds **Y** and **Z**?

iii) From the information above, deduce which of the structures referred to in a) is that of alkene **X**.

iv) Name this isomer.

c) A further isomer of **X** belongs to a different homologous series from those referred to in a).

i) Draw its structural formula.

ii) Give its systematic name.

iii) Describe a test which would distinguish this isomer from the others.

15. One of the most important feedstocks in the petrochemical industry is ethene. The following flow chart gives some uses of ethene.

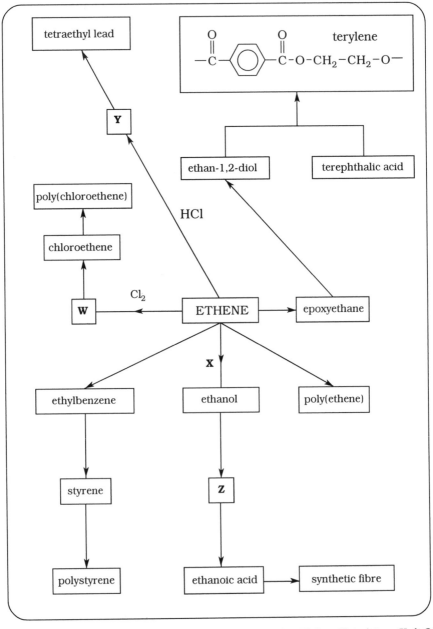

a) State **one** way in which ethene is formed in the petrochemical industry.

b) Name product **W** and reactant **X**.

c) Draw the full structural formulae for compounds **Y** and **Z**.

d) i) Name the kind of polymerisation which takes place in the formation of poly(ethene), poly(chloroethene) and polystyrene.

ii) A structural formula for styrene is shown.

$$CH=CH_2$$

Draw the structure of part of the polystyrene chain which is formed by **three** monomer units linking together.

e) i) Name the kind of polymerisation which takes place in the formation of terylene.

ii) Draw structural formulae for terephthalic acid and ethan-1,2-diol.

16.

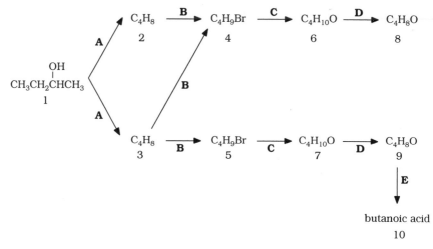

a) Is compound 1 a primary, secondary or tertiary alcohol?

b) Draw structural formulae for the isomeric compounds 2 and 3.

c) What reagents would be used in steps **A**, **B**, **D** and **E**?

d) Draw structural formulae for isomeric compounds 8 and 9.

e) Which of compounds 6 and 7 is an isomer of compound 1?

Unit 3   Chemical Reactions

Exercise 3.1   The chemical industry

1. **The chemical industry** is the only major sector of the UK manufacturing industry which **makes a positive contributrion to the UK's balance of trade with the rest of the world**.
    What is meant by the part of the sentence shown in bold?

2. Stages in the industrial manufacture of a new product can include
    a) research,
    b) pilot study,
    c) scaling up,
    d) production,
    e) review.
    Describe what is involved at each stage.

3. Select **two** products of the chemical industry and for each product describe the steps involved in the manufacturing processes.

4. a) In the chemical industry, what is meant by a feedstock?
    b) What is the most important factor in deciding which feedstock to use?

5. a) In the chemical industry, what is meant by a raw material?
    b) Consider the following list.
        air, ethene, ammonia, water, oil, benzene, coal, plastics, fertilisers, sulphuric acid, iron ore, natural gas, aluminium oxide, sodium hydroxide.
        Which of the above can be classified as a raw material?

6. The cost of energy is of major importance to the chemical industry.
    Describe **one** way by which energy costs can be kept down.

7. Chemical manufacturing can be organised as a batch or a continuous process.
   a) Describe the two different types of operation.
   b) State **two** advantages associated with each.
   c) Give **two** chemicals manufactured by each type of operation.

8. Give **two** examples of steps taken by the chemical industry to improve the safety of
   a) those who work in the industry,
   b) those who live near to a chemical plant.

9. Give **two** examples of steps taken by the chemical industry to reduce damage to the environment.

10. Describe **three** factors which can influence the location of a chemical plant.

11. Capital costs, fixed costs and variable costs are all incurred in operating a chemical plant.
    a) What is meant by each type of cost?
    b) Give **two** examples of each type of cost.
    c) How does increasing the output of a chemical plant affect each type of cost?

12. Most of the UK chemical industry is **capital rather than labour intensive**.
    a) What is meant by the part of the sentence shown in bold?
    b) How does the sales income per employee for a capital intensive company compare with that for a labour intensive company?

13. In the Haber Process, increasing pressure increases the yield of ammonia.
    Why then is the process carried out at 200 atmospheres pressure and **not** at 400 atmospheres pressure?

14. Ammonia is prepared by the Haber Process.

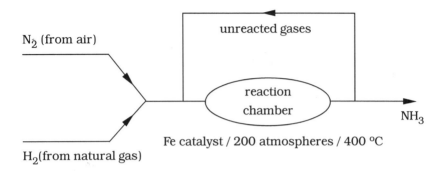

Based on the diagram,
a) give **three** reasons why this route to ammonia is economically effective,
b) give **one** other reason, not illustrated by the Haber Process, why a particular industrial route to a chemical product may be chosen.

Exercise 3.2

Hess's law

1. The following three reactions can be used to confirm Hess's law.

$$KOH(s) \rightarrow KOH(aq) \qquad \Delta H = \mathbf{a}$$
$$KOH(s) + HCl(aq) \rightarrow KCl(aq) + H_2O(l) \qquad \Delta H = \mathbf{b}$$
$$KOH(aq) + HCl(aq) \rightarrow KCl(aq) + H_2O(l) \qquad \Delta H = \mathbf{c}$$

a) Use Hess's law to write an equation to show the relationship between **a**, **b**, and **c**.

b) Write in words a statement of Hess's law.

2.

Enthalpy change	ΔH / kJ mol^{-1}
$C(s) \rightarrow C(g)$	+715
$C_3H_8(g) + 5O_2(g) \rightarrow 3CO_2(g) + 4H_2O(l)$	−2220
$3C(s) + 4H_2(g) \rightarrow C_3H_8(g)$	−104

Calculate the enthalpy change for the reaction:
$$3C(g) + 4H_2(g) \rightarrow C_3H_8(g)$$

3.

Enthalpy change	ΔH / kJ mol^{-1}
$RbCl(s) \rightarrow Rb^+(aq) + Cl^-(aq)$	+17
$Rb^+(g) \rightarrow Rb^+(aq)$	−301
$Cl^-(g) \rightarrow Cl^-(aq)$	−364

Calculate the enthalpy of lattice breaking for rubidium chloride:
$$RbCl(s) \rightarrow Rb^+(g) + Cl^-(g)$$

4.

$$NaOH(s) \rightarrow NaOH(aq) \qquad \Delta H = ?$$
$$NaOH(s) + HCl(aq) \rightarrow NaCl(aq) + H_2O(l) \quad \Delta H = -105 \text{kJ mol}^{-1}$$
$$NaOH(aq) + HCl(aq) \rightarrow NaCl(aq) + H_2O(l) \quad \Delta H = -65.8 \text{ kJ mol}^{-1}$$

Calculate the enthalpy of solution of sodium hydroxide.

5. Use the information below to calculate the enthalpy of combustion of carbon monoxide.

$$2C(s) \quad + \quad O_2(g) \quad \rightarrow \quad 2CO(g) \quad \Delta H \ = \ -216 \ kJ$$
$$C(s) \quad + \quad O_2(g) \quad \rightarrow \quad CO_2(g) \quad \Delta H \ = \ -394 \ kJ$$

6.

Enthalpy change	ΔH / kJ mol^{-1}
$CH_2Cl_2(g) \ + \ O_2(g) \ \rightarrow \ CO_2(g) \ + \ 2HCl(g)$	-446
$C(s) \ + \ O_2(g) \ \rightarrow \ CO_2(g)$	-394
$H_2(g) \ + \ Cl_2(g) \ \rightarrow \ 2HCl(g)$	-184

Calculate the enthalpy change for the reaction:

$$C(s) \quad + \quad H_2(g) \quad + \quad Cl_2(g) \quad \rightarrow \quad CH_2Cl_2(g)$$

7. Calculate the enthalpy change for the reaction:

$$C_2H_4(g) \quad + \quad H_2(g) \quad \rightarrow \quad C_2H_6(g)$$

Use the enthalpies of combustion of hydrogen, ethene (C_2H_4) and ethane (C_2H_6) given in your data booklet.

8. The enthalpy of formation of propan-1-ol is the enthalpy change for the reaction:

$$3C(s) \quad + \quad 4H_2(g) \quad + \quad \tfrac{1}{2}O_2(g) \quad \rightarrow \quad C_3H_7OH(l)$$

$$\text{propan-1-ol}$$

Calculate the enthalpy of formation of propan-1-ol using the enthalpies of combustion of carbon, hydrogen and propan-1-ol given in your data booklet.

9. Use the enthalpies of combustion given in your data booklet to calculate the enthalpy change for the reaction:

$$2C(s) \quad + \quad 3H_2(g) \quad \rightarrow \quad C_2H_6(g)$$

10. The enthalpy of formation of cyclohexane (C_6H_{12}) is the enthalpy change for the reaction:

$$6C(s) \ + \ 6H_2(g) \ \rightarrow \ C_6H_{12}(l)$$

Use the enthalpies of combustion given in your data booklet to calculate the enthalpy of formation of cyclohexane.

(Take the enthalpy of combustion of cyclohexane to be -3920 kJ mol^{-1}.)

11. The enthalpy of formation of butane is the enthalpy change for the reaction:

$$4C(s) \ + \ 5H_2(g) \ \rightarrow \ C_4H_{10}(g)$$

Calculate the enthalpy change for the complete combustion of butane using the enthalpy of formation of butane and the enthalpies of combustion of carbon and hydrogen given in your data booklet.

12. The enthalpy of formation of ethanol is the enthalpy change for the reaction:

$$2C(s) \ + \ 3H_2(g) \ + \ \tfrac{1}{2}O_2(g) \ \rightarrow \ C_2H_5OH(l)$$

Using enthalpies of combustion given in your data booklet, calculate the enthalpy of formation of ethanol.

13. $CH_3NHNH_2(l) \ + \ {}^5/_2O_2(g) \ \rightarrow \ CO_2(g) \ + \ 3H_2O(l) \ + \ N_2(g)$

methylhydrazine $\hspace{4cm} \Delta H \ = \ -1305kJ$

Using this information, together with the enthalpies of combustion in your data booklet, calculate the enthalpy change for the reaction:

$$C(s) \ + \ 3H_2(g) \ + \ N_2(g) \ \rightarrow \ CH_3NHNH_2(l)$$

14. Use the enthalpy changes given in the table to calculate the enthalpy of combustion of the gas diborane, B_2H_6.

Enthalpy change	ΔH / kJ mol^{-1}
$2B(s) \ + \ 3H_2(g) \ \rightarrow \ B_2H_6(g)$	+32
$H_2(g) \ + \ {}^1/_2O_2(g) \ \rightarrow \ H_2O(l)$	−286
$2B(s) \ + \ {}^3/_2O_2(g) \ \rightarrow \ B_2O_3(s)$	−1225

Exercise 3.3   Equilibrium

1. Ozone, O_3, may be produced in the laboratory by the action of electrical discharge on dry oxygen.

$$3O_2(g) \rightleftharpoons 2O_3(g) \qquad \Delta H = +285.5 \text{ kJ mol}^{-1}$$

Predict how the equilibrium would be affected by
a)   an increase in pressure,
b)   an increase in temperature.

2. The reaction

$$ICl_3(l) \quad + \quad Cl_2(g) \quad \rightleftharpoons \quad ICl_5(s)$$
     (brown liquid)   (yellow solid)

is exothermic for the formation of ICl_5.
Predict what would be **seen** to happen to a mixture at equilibrium if
a)   more chlorine was added,
b)   the temperature was increased,
c)   the pressure was decreased,
d)   a catalyst was added.

3. Consider the following equilibrium.

$$N_2(g) \quad + \quad 2O_2(g) \quad \rightleftharpoons \quad 2NO_2(g) \qquad \Delta H = +180 \text{ kJ mol}^{-1}$$

Predict how the equilibrium concentration of nitrogen dioxide would be affected by
a)   increasing the temperature,
b)   decreasing the pressure,
c)   decreasing the concentration of oxygen.

4. Consider the following equilibrium.

$$N_2O_4(g) \quad \rightleftharpoons \quad 2NO_2(g) \qquad \Delta H \text{ is } +ve$$
     (pale yellow)   (dark brown)

Explain what would be **seen** if the equilibrium mixture was
a)   placed in a freezing mixture,
b)   compressed.

5. Synthesis gas, a mixture of hydrogen and carbon monoxide, is prepared as shown.

$$CH_4(g) + H_2O(g) \rightleftharpoons 3H_2(g) + CO(g)$$

a) An increase in temperature increases the yield of synthesis gas. What information does this give about the enthalpy change for the forward reaction?

b) Explain how a change in pressure will affect the composition of the equilibrium mixture.

c) i) State how the rate of formation of synthesis gas will be affected by the use of a catalyst.

   ii) State how the composition of the equilibrium mixture will be affected by the use of a catalyst.

6. Ethanol is produced industrially at 70 atmospheres pressure and 300 °C.

$$C_2H_4(g) + H_2O(g) \rightleftharpoons C_2H_5OH(g) \qquad \Delta H = -46 \text{ kJmol}^{-1}$$

a) Explain why the yield of ethanol is increased by
   i) decreasing the temperature,
   ii) increasing the pressure.

b) Suggest why the industrial process is **not** carried out
   i) at temperatures much below 300 °C,
   ii) at pressures much above 70 atmospheres.

7. Ammonia gas dissolves in water to form an alkaline solution.

$$NH_3(g) + H_2O(l) \rightleftharpoons NH_4^+(aq) + OH^-(aq) \qquad \Delta H = -30.6 \text{ kJ mol}^{-1}$$

Predict how each of the following changes would affect the equilibrium position.

a) increasing the temperature

b) increasing the pressure

c) adding an aqueous acid

8.

Reaction (1): $H_2(g) + I_2(g) \rightleftharpoons 2HI(g)$

Reaction (2): $2CO(g) + O_2(g) \rightleftharpoons 2CO_2(g)$

Reaction (3): $CH_3OH(g) \rightleftharpoons CO(g) + 2H_2(g)$

Reaction (4): $C(s) + CO_2(g) \rightleftharpoons 2CO(g)$

a) For each of the above reactions decide whether an increase in pressure will
   i) shift the position of eqilibrium to the left,
   ii) have no effect on the equilibrium position,
   iii) shift the position of equilibrium to the right.

b) In reaction (1), the forward reaction is exothermic.
   What effect, if any, will an increase in temperature have on the equilibrium position?

9. In Britain, the main source of magnesium is sea water. One stage in the production of magnesium is shown in the diagram.

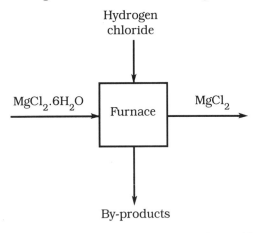

In the furnace, the water of crystallisation in the $MgCl_2.6H_2O$ is removed by heating. However this can cause the formation of magnesium oxide.

$MgCl_2.6H_2O \rightleftharpoons MgO + 2HCl + 5H_2O$

a) Which chemical is used to prevent this?

b) Explain how this chemical prevents the formation of magnesium oxide.

10. The major reactions in three industrial processes may be represented as follows.

Process	Equation	Temp. / °C	Press. / atm	ΔH / kJmol^{-1}
A	$N_2(g) + 3H_2(g) \rightleftharpoons 2NH_3(g)$	400	200	-92
B	$4NH_3(g) + 5O_2(g) \rightleftharpoons 4NO_2(g) + 6H_2O(g)$	800	4	-909
C	$2SO_2(g) + O_2(g) \rightleftharpoons 2SO_3(g)$	400	1	-98

a) Justify the use of high pressure in process **A** but **not** process **B**.

b) Explain whether the temperatures employed in all these reactions are consistent with the enthalpy changes involved.

11. When chlorine is dissolved in water the following equilibrium is set up.

$$Cl_2(aq) + H_2O(l) \rightleftharpoons 2H^+(aq) + ClO^-(aq) + Cl^-(aq)$$

The hypochlorite ion, ClO^-, is responsible for the bleaching action of the solution.

What effect on the bleaching efficiency of a solution of chlorine in water would each of the following have?

a) adding dilute nitric acid

b) adding sodium chloride crystals

c) adding sodium sulphate crystals

d) adding potassium hydroxide solution

12. The test tube is shaken until no further change is visible.

Explain what is happening at the interface

a) after equilibrium is established,

b) immediately after **more** chloroform is added.

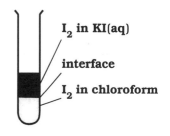

I$_2$ in KI(aq)

interface

I$_2$ in chloroform

13. Calcium sulphate is only sparingly soluble in water. It forms an equilibrium mixture.

$$CaSO_4(s) \rightleftharpoons Ca^{2+}(aq) + SO_4^{2-}(aq)$$

Predict how the equilibrium mixture would be affected by adding

a) dilute sulphuric acid,

b) aqueous barium chloride.

(You may wish to refer to the solubility table in your data booklet.)

14. Consider the following industrial processes.

Contact Process $2SO_2(g) + O_2(g) \rightleftharpoons 2SO_3(g)$ ΔH is +ve

Haber Process $N_2(g) + 3H_2(g) \rightleftharpoons 2NH_3(g)$ ΔH is +ve

a) Explain which way the equilibrium positions would move with increasing temperature.

b) Suggest why the Contact Process uses atmospheric pressure whereas the Haber Process uses pressures in excess of 200 atmospheres.

c) Suggest **one** advantage and **one** disadvantage of increasing the pressure in the Haber Process beyond 200 atmospheres.

15. The industrial preparation of methanol involves the combination of carbon monoxide and hydrogen.

$$CO(g) + 2H_2(g) \rightleftharpoons CH_3OH(g)$$

The following curves show the percentages of methanol in the equilibrium mixture under different conditions.

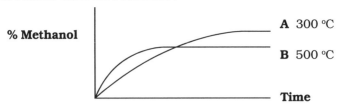

% Methanol

A 300 °C

B 500 °C

Time

a) In industry, the reaction is usually carried out at 300 atmospheres pressure.

Explain the use of high pressure.

b) i) Is the reaction which produces methanol exothermic or endothermic?

ii) Explain your answer.

16. When bromine is added to water, a brown solution is formed.
    The following equilibrium is set up.

    $$Br_2(aq) + H_2O(l) \rightleftharpoons Br^-(aq) + BrO^-(aq) + 2H^+(aq)$$

    Explain what would happen to the **colour** of bromine solution on the addition of

    (a) hydrochloric acid,

    (b) silver nitrate solution.

17. The table below gives information about the percentage yields of ammonia obtained in the Haber process under different conditions.

Pressure / atmospheres	Temperature / $^{\circ}C$			
	200	300	400	500
10	50.7	14.7	3.9	1.2
100	81.7	52.5	25.2	10.6
200	89.0	66.7	38.8	18.3
300	89.9	71.0	47.0	24.4
400	94.6	79.7	55.4	31.9
600	95.4	84.2	65.2	42.3

   a) From the table, which combination of temperature and pressure gives the highest yield of ammonia?

   b) The equation for the main reaction of the Haber process is

   $$N_2(g) + 3H_2(g) \rightleftharpoons 2NH_3(g) \quad \Delta H \text{ is negative}$$

   Use this information to explain the effect of

   i) pressure,

   ii) temperature,

   on the equilibrium yield of ammonia.

   c) In practice, the conditions used are 400 $^{\circ}C$ and 200 atmospheres. Explain why these conditions are used rather than those which give the highest yield.

Exercise 3.4   The pH scale

1. Pure water conducts electricity, but only very slightly.
    a) State the concentration of hydrogen ions, $H^+(aq)$, in pure water.
    b) How does the concentration of hydroxide ions, $OH^-(aq)$, compare
        with the concentration of hydrogen ions?

2. State the pH of the solutions with each of the following hydrogen ion
    concentrations.
    a) $[H^+(aq)]$ = 1×10^{-3} mol l^{-1}
    b) $[H^+(aq)]$ = 1×10^{-9} mol l^{-1}
    c) $[H^+(aq)]$ = 1 mol l^{-1}
    d) $[H^+(aq)]$ = 1×10^{-13} mol l^{-1}

3. State the concentration of hydroxide ions in solutions with each of the
    following hydrogen ion concentrations.
    a) $[H^+(aq)]$ = 1×10^{-3} mol l^{-1}
    b) $[H^+(aq)]$ = 1×10^{-14} mol l^{-1}
    c) $[H^+(aq)]$ = 1×10^{-6} mol l^{-1}
    d) $[H^+(aq)]$ = 1×10^{-15} mol l^{-1}

4. State the concentration of hydrogen ions in solutions with each of the
    following hydroxide ion concentrations.
    a) $[OH^-(aq)]$ = 1×10^{-2} mol l^{-1}
    b) $[OH^-(aq)]$ = 1×10^{-1} mol l^{-1}
    c) $[OH^-(aq)]$ = 1×10^{-6} mol l^{-1}
    d) $[OH^-(aq)]$ = 1×10^{-7} mol l^{-1}

5. State the concentration of hydroxide ions in solutions with each of the
    following pH values.
    a) 2
    b) 7
    c) 0
    d) 14

Exercise 3.5   Strong and weak acids and bases

1. The terms weak and strong and dilute and concentrated are often
    confused.
    a) Explain clearly the difference between
        i)   a dilute acid and a concentrated acid,
        ii) a weak acid and a strong acid.
    b) Give **one** example of
        i)   a weak acid,
        ii) a strong acid.
    c) As a strong acid is diluted, state what happens to
        i)   the concentration of hydrogen ions, $H^+(aq)$,
        ii) the number of hydrogen ions, $H^+(aq)$.

2.

Acid	pH of 2 mol l^{-1} solution
A CCl_3COOH	0.50
B $CHCl_2COOH$	0.90

    a) i)   Which is the stronger acid?
        ii) Explain.
    b) Which has the higher conductivity?
    c) Which reacts faster with magnesium?
    d) 25 cm^3 of 2 mol l^{-1} sodium hydroxide solution is required to
        neutralise a fixed volume of acid **A**.
        i)   What volume of the same alkali would be required to neutralise
             the same volume of acid **B**?
        ii) Explain your answer.

3. Explain what happens to the pH of ammonia solution when ammonium
    chloride is added.

4. Explain what happens to the pH of water when carbon dioxide is
    bubbled through.

5. A pupil carried out three experiments to compare the properties of sodium hydroxide solution with ammonia solution.

Experiment	Sodium hydroxide solution	Ammonia solution
pH	higher	lower
Conductivity	higher	lower
Volume of dilute acid required to neutralise 25 cm^3 of alkali	same	same

a) Write an equation to show why ammonia is a weak base.

b) Explain why the concentrations of the two alkalis must be kept the same in each of the experiments.

c) Explain the results of each experiment.

6. Benzoic acid is a weak acid.

benzoic acid   benzoate ion

Explain what happens to the pH of a solution of the acid when sodium benzoate is added.

Exercise 3.6   The pH of salt solutions

1.   When sodium carbonate dissolves in water the pH increases.
     Explain this change.

2.

$$C_{12}H_{25} - \langle \bigcirc \rangle - SO_3^- \, Na^+$$

sodium sulphonate

A sodium sulphonate solution has a pH greater than 7.
a)   What does this indicate about the sulphonic acid from which it is
     made?
b)   Explain why the sodium sulphonate solution is alkaline.

3.   Salts can have a pH less than 7, a pH equal to 7 or a pH greater than 7.
     Make a table with the above headings, and place each of the following
     salts in the correct column in the table.

     sodium sulphite, potassium chloride, lithium carbonate,
     ammonium sulphate, potassium nitrate, ammonium nitrate,
     sodium ethanoate, lithium sulphate, ammonium chloride.

4.   Solutions of the salt potassium cyanide (KCN) are alkaline.
     a)   What is the formula of the acid from which potassium cyanide is
          derived.
     b)   Is it a strong or weak acid?
     c)   Explain why potassium cyanide solution is alkaline.

Exercise 3.7   Oxidising and reducing agents

1. For each of the following reactions, combine the oxidation and reduction steps to form a balanced ionic equation.

a) $Al(s) \rightarrow Al^{3+}(aq) + 3e^-$

    $2H^+(aq) + 2e^- \rightarrow H_2(g)$

b) $Ce^{4+}(aq) + e^- \rightarrow Ce^{3+}(aq)$

    $2Br^-(aq) \rightarrow Br_2(aq) + 2e^-$

c) $Cu(s) \rightarrow Cu^{2+}(aq) + 2e^-$

    $Ag^+(aq) + e^- \rightarrow Ag(s)$

d) $MnO_4^-(aq) + 8H^+(aq) + 5e^- \rightarrow Mn^{2+}(aq) + 4H_2O(l)$

    $Fe^{2+}(aq) \rightarrow Fe^{3+}(aq) + e^-$

e) $Cr_2O_7^{2-}(aq) + 14H^+(aq) + 6e^- \rightarrow 2Cr^{3+}(aq) + 7H_2O(l)$

    $Sn^{2+}(aq) \rightarrow Sn^{4+}(aq) + 2e^-$

2. For each of the following reactions, write an ion-electron equation for the oxidation and reduction.

a) $Cl_2(aq) + 2Fe^{2+}(aq) \rightarrow 2Cl^-(aq) + 2Fe^{3+}(aq)$

b) $Zn(s) + Cu^{2+}(aq) \rightarrow Zn^{2+}(aq) + Cu(s)$

c) $Mg(s) + 2H^+(aq) \rightarrow Mg^{2+}(aq) + H_2(g)$

d) $Cl_2(g) + 2KBr(aq) \rightarrow Br_2(aq) + 2KCl(aq)$

e) $2Na(s) + H_2(g) \rightarrow 2NaH(s)$

f) $2Na_2S_2O_3(aq) + I_2(aq) \rightarrow 2NaI(aq) + Na_2S_4O_6(aq)$

g) $5CrCl_2(aq) + KMnO_4(aq) + 8HCl(aq)$

        $\rightarrow 5CrCl_3(aq) + KCl(aq) + MnCl_2(aq) + 4H_2O(l)$

3. For each of the following reactions, write an ion-electron equation for the oxidation and reduction. Combine the oxidations and reductions to form the redox reactions.

a) Sodium sulphite reduces iodine to iodide ions.

b) Potassium iodide reduces chlorine solution.

c) Potassium permanganate oxidises hydrochloric acid to chlorine.

d) In acid solution, potassium dichromate oxidises iron(II) sulphate to iron(III) sulphate.

e) In acid solution, potassium permanganate oxidises sodium bromide.

4. Write a balanced ion-electron equation for each of the following reactions.

a) $\quad SO_3^{2-} \rightarrow SO_4^{2-}$

b) $\quad MnO_4^- \rightarrow Mn^{2+}$

c) $\quad IO_3^- \rightarrow I_2$

d) $\quad ClO_3^- \rightarrow Cl_2$

e) $\quad PbO_2 \rightarrow Pb^{2+}$

f) $\quad XeO_3 \rightarrow Xe$

g) $\quad ClO^- \rightarrow Cl^-$

Exercise 3.8   Redox titrations

1. Iron(II) ions react with dichromate ions in acidic solution.

    $$6Fe^{2+}(aq) + Cr_2O_7^{2-}(aq) + 14H^+(aq) \rightarrow 6Fe^{3+}(aq) + 2Cr^{3+}(aq) + 7H_2O(l)$$

    Calculate the amount of iron(II) ions, in moles, which will react completely with 250 cm^3 of dichromate solution, concentration 0.1mol l^{-1}.

2. Permanganate ions react with hydrogen peroxide in acidic solution.

    $$2MnO_4^-(aq) + 6H^+(aq) + 5H_2O_2(aq) \rightarrow 2Mn^{2+}(aq) + 8H_2O(l) + 5O_2(aq)$$

    25 cm^3 of hydrogen peroxide solution reacted with 16 cm^3 of permanganate solution, concentration 0.1 mol l^{-1}.
    Calculate the concentration of the hydrogen peroxide solution.

3. Dichromate ions react with ethanol in acidic solution.

    $$2Cr_2O_7^{2-}(aq) + 3C_2H_5OH(aq) + 16H^+(aq)$$
    $$\rightarrow 3CH_3COOH(aq) + 4Cr^{3+}(aq) + 11H_2O(l)$$

    It was found that 12.5 cm^3 of 0.1 mol l^{-1} potassium dichromate solution was required to oxidise the ethanol in a 1 cm^3 sample of wine.
    Calculate the mass of ethanol in the 1 cm^3 wine sample.

4. A cigarette lighter flint contained cerium. It was dissolved in 30 cm^3 of dilute sulphuric acid, and heated with a catalyst to produce a solution containing $Ce^{4+}(aq)$ ions.
    It was found that 4.85 cm^3 of iron(II) sulphate solution, concentration 0.05 mol l^{-1}, was required to reduce 10 cm^3 of the $Ce^{4+}(aq)$ solution.

Equations				
$Fe^{2+}(aq)$	$\rightarrow$	$Fe^{3+}(aq)$	$+$	e^-
$Ce^{4+}(aq)$ $+$ e^-	$\rightarrow$	$Ce^{3+}(aq)$		

    Calculate the mass of cerium in the flint.
    (Take the relative atomic mass of cerium to be 140.)

5. The chlorine levels in swimming pools can be determined by titrating samples against acidified iron(II) sulphate solution. The reaction taking place is:

$$Cl_2(aq) \quad + \quad 2Fe^{2+}(aq) \quad \rightarrow \quad 2Cl^-(aq) \quad + \quad 2Fe^{3+}(aq)$$

A 100 cm^3 sample of water from a swimming pool required 24.9 cm^3 of iron(II) sulphate, concentration 2.82 mol l^{-1}, to reach the end-point. Calculate the chlorine concentration, in g l^{-1}, in the swimming pool water.

6. In an experiment to measure the concentration of ozone, O_3, in the air in a Scottish city, 10^5 litres of air were bubbled through a solution of potassium iodide. Ozone reacts with potassium iodide releasing iodine.

$$2KI(aq) \quad + \quad O_3(g) \quad + \quad H_2O(l) \quad \rightarrow \quad I_2(aq) \quad + \quad O_2(g) \quad + \quad 2KOH(aq)$$

The iodine formed was completely oxidised by 22.5 cm^3 of sodium thiosulphate solution, concentration 0.01 mol l^{-1}.

$$I_2(aq) \quad + \quad 2S_2O_3^{2-}(aq) \quad \rightarrow \quad 2I^-(aq) \quad + \quad S_4O_6^{2-}(aq)$$

Calculate the volume of ozone in 1 litre of air.

(Take the volume of one mole of ozone to be 24 litres.)

7. The percentage purity of iron(II) salts can be found by titration with acidified potassium permanganate solution.

The following relationship can be used to calculate the percentage purity of a salt.   percentage purity   = $\dfrac{\text{mass of pure salt}}{\text{mass of impure salt}}$ x 100

A pupil was given 1.55 g of impure iron(II) sulphate, $FeSO_4.7H_2O$, and used this to prepare 250 cm^3 of solution for the titration.

It was found that 9.5 cm^3 of acidified potassium permanganate, concentration 0.01 mol l^{-1}, was required to oxidise 25 cm^3 of the iron(II) sulphate solution.

Equations
$Fe^{2+}(aq) \quad \rightarrow \quad Fe^{3+}(aq) \quad + \quad e^-$
$MnO_4^-(aq) \quad + \quad 8H^+(aq) \quad + \quad 5e^- \quad \rightarrow \quad Mn^{2+}(aq) \quad + \quad 4H_2O(aq)$

Calculate the mass of pure iron(II) sulphate and thus find the percentage purity of the iron(II) sulphate salt.

Exercise 3.9   Electrolysis

1. A sample of molten nickel(II) chloride was electrolysed using a current of
    0.4 A for a time of 16 min 5 s.
    Calculate the mass of nickel which was formed.

2. Calcium is manufactured by the electrolysis of molten calcium chloride.
    Calculate the mass of calcium which is produced by a current of 20 A
    passing for 32 min 10 s.

3. In the Downs Process, sodium is extracted from sodium chloride by
    electrolysis.
    Calculate the mass of sodium formed when a current of 30 000 A flows
    for 10 min.

4. Aluminium is extracted from aluminium oxide by electrolysis. A typical
    cell current is 150 000 A.
    Calculate the mass of aluminium which can be produced per minute in
    such a cell.

5. A current of 0.4 A is passed through copper(II) sulphate solution,
    concentration 1 mol l^{-1}.
    Calculate, to the nearest second, the time required to deposit 0.16 g of
    copper on the negative electrode.

6. In an industrial process, a current of 10 000 A was passed through a gold
    solution for 25 min producing 10.21 kg of gold metal.
    Calculate the charge on the gold ions in the solution.

In questions 7 to 9 take the volume of one mole of the gas to be 23.0 litres.

7. Chlorine can be produced by the electrolysis of brine in the Castner-Kellner cell.
    Calculate the volume of chlorine produced per minute using a current of 30 000 A.

8. Dilute sulphuric acid is electrolysed using a current of 1.15 A for a time of 50 min.
    Calculate the volume of gas which will be given off at the negative electrode.

9. The same quantity of electricity is passed through solutions of silver nitrate and sulphuric acid.
    If 0.54 g of silver is deposited from the silver nitate solution, calculate the volume of hydrogen which will be produced from the sulphuric acid.

10. Calculate the maximum mass of copper which could be deposited by 6.02×10^{22} electrons in the electrolysis of copper(II) chloride solution.

11. When a current of 1 A was passed for 1 hour 20 min, 0.6 g of a metal was produced.
    Given that the metal is in Group 2 of the Periodic Table, calculate the relative atomic mass.

12. Calculate the number of electrons required to produce 0.5 g of hydrogen gas at the negative electrode during the electrolysis of dilute acid.

13. Cells containing mercury(II) nitrate and silver(I) nitrate are connected in series.
    Calculate the mass of mercury which would be deposited by a quantity of electricity sufficient to deposit 0.324 g of silver.

Exercise 3.10   Radioactivity

1. Alpha, beta and gamma radiation have different penetrating properties.
    Name the type of radiation which is
    a)   able to penetrate 5 cm of lead,
    b)   stopped by a sheet of paper,
    c)   stopped by a sheet of aluminium.

2. The following experiment was carried out using a radioisotope which
    emitted alpha, beta and gamma radiation.

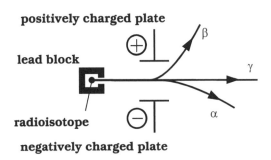

    a)   i)   Why is the radioisotope surrounded by a thick lead block?
         ii) Explain the paths taken by the three different types of radiation.
    b)   Why are the nuclei of radioisotopes unstable?

3. Smoke detectors use the alpha radiation from americium-241 to ionise
    the air in a small chamber. When smoke is present, the conductivity of
    the air is changed and a buzzer is activated.
    The half-life of americium-241 is 433 years.
    Give **two** reasons why americium-241 is a suitable radioisotope for
    use in an overhead smoke detector.

4. The isotope $_{27}^{60}$Co has a half-life of 5.3 years. and is used to supply
    gamma radiation from outside the body of a patient.
    Give **two** reasons why this isotope would **not** be suitable for use inside
    the body.

5. Carbon-14 dating can be used to estimate the age of clothing found in archaeological "digs".

   a) Describe how the age of some remains can be determined by this method.

   b) Why can this method of dating **not** be used to find the age of diamonds in jewellery?

   c) Why can this method of dating **not** be used for remains which are more than 50 000 years old?

6. The following reactions can occur when uranium-235 is bombarded with neutrons.

$$^{235}_{92}U + ^{1}_{0}n \rightarrow ^{236}_{92}U$$

$$^{236}_{92}U \rightarrow ^{90}_{36}Kr + ^{144}_{56}Ba + 2^{1}_{0}n$$

   a) What name is given to the process in which a heavy nucleus splits into lighter ones?

   b) Why is a lage amount of energy released by these reactions?

   c) Give **two** ways of using this energy.

7. Uranium-238 is a naturally occuring radioisotope found in rocks.
   By referring to the data booklet, explain why

   a) large amounts of uranium-238 can be found but only traces of protactinium-234 occur,

   b) lead-206 is often found with uranium-238.

8. $$^{2}_{1}H + ^{2}_{1}H \rightarrow ^{3}_{2}He + ^{1}_{0}n$$

   a) Name this type of reaction.

   b) Where do reactions of this type occur.

9. a) What is meant by a radioactive tracer.

   b) Give **one** use for a radioactive tracer.

10. Radioisotopes are used in a wide variety of ways.

    a) Name a radioisotope used in medicine and give its use.

    b) Describe an industrial use for a radioisotope.

Exercise 3.11   Nuclear equations

1. $^{225}_{88}\text{Ra} \quad \rightarrow \quad ^{225}_{89}\text{Ac} \quad + \quad \mathbf{y}$

       $^{217}_{85}\text{At} \quad \rightarrow \quad ^{213}_{83}\text{Bi} \quad + \quad \mathbf{z}$

   State the mass and charge of each of the particles **y** and **z**, and identify
   them.

2.   Identify the isotope which is formed when
   a)   sodium-24 emits beta particles,
   b)   plutonium-242 emits alpha particles.

3.   Write a nuclear equation for
   a) α-decay of $^{210}_{84}\text{Po}$,

   b) β-decay of tritium, $^{3}_{1}\text{H}$,

   c) α-decay of $^{226}_{88}\text{Ra}$,

   d) β-decay of $^{90}_{38}\text{Sr}$.

4.   a)   Write a nuclear equation to show what happens when
            ^{232}Th undergoes α-emission.
   b)   Show, by calculation, that the neutron to proton ratio has increased.

5.   Part of a radioactive decay series is shown below.

            β-decay β-decay
       $^{231}_{90}\text{Th} \quad \rightarrow \quad$ isotope **X** $\quad \rightarrow \quad$ isotope **Y** $\quad \rightarrow \quad ^{227}_{90}\text{Th}$

   a)   Identify isotopes **X** and **Y**.
   b)   Which type of decay occurs between isotope **X** and isotope **Y**?

6.   An atom loses successively an alpha particle, a beta particle and a gamma
   ray. What net effect would this have on the parent nucleus?

7. $^{239}_{92}U$ can be made by bombarding $^{238}_{92}U$ with neutrons.

a) Write a nuclear equation for this reaction.

b) The following diagram shows the $^{239}_{92}U$ radioactive decay series.

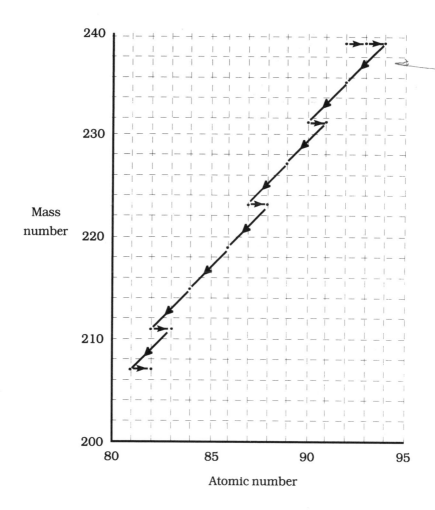

Atomic number

Use this information to find the total number of

i) α-emissions,

ii) β-emissions.

8. **P** is a radioisotope which undergoes transitions as follows.

$$\begin{array}{ccccccc} & \beta\text{-emission} & & \beta\text{-emission} & & \alpha\text{-emission} & \\ \mathbf{P} & \rightarrow & \mathbf{Q} & \rightarrow & \mathbf{R} & \rightarrow & \mathbf{S} \end{array}$$

If the atomic number of **P** is 88, and its mass number is 228, what are the atomic number and mass number of isotope **S**?

9. The radioactive isotope $^{227}_{87}$Fr decays to form a stable isotope $^{b}_{a}\mathbf{X}$ by the following sequence of emissions.

$$\alpha, \quad \alpha, \quad \beta, \quad \alpha, \quad \beta$$

Identify element **X** and write values for **a** and **b**.

10. What is the source of ^{206}Pb, if it is formed by α-emission followed by β-emission?

Exercise 3.12   Artificial radioisotopes

1. Many radioisotopes are made by bombarding stable atoms with alpha particles, neutrons or protons.
    a) Why are neutrons widely used for producing radioisotopes?
    b) Why are beta particles not used to produce radioisotopes?

2. Complete each of the following nuclear equations and identify **R** and **S**.
    a) ^6_3Li + ^1_0n $\rightarrow$ ^3_1H + **R**
    b) $^{238}_{92}\text{U}$ + ^4_2He $\rightarrow$ $^{239}_{94}\text{Pu}$ + **3S**

3. State the mass and charge of each of the particles **x** and **y**, and identify them.

    a) $^{14}_7\text{N}$ + ^4_2He $\rightarrow$ $^{17}_8\text{O}$ + **x**

    b) ^6_3Li + **y** $\rightarrow$ ^3_1H + ^4_2He

4. a) $^{10}_5\text{B}$ + ^1_0n $\rightarrow$ $^p_q\textbf{X}$ + ^4_2He

        Identify element **X** and write values for **p** and **q**.

    b) $^a_b\textbf{Y}$ + ^1_0n $\rightarrow$ $^{24}_{11}\text{Na}$

        Identify element **Y** and write values for **a** and **b**.

5. When, during bombardment, an atom of aluminium-27 captures a neutron, emission of an α-particle occurs and a radioactive isotope, **X**, is formed. **X** then decays by β-emission to form a stable isotope **Y**. Write nuclear equations to illustrate these two reactions and identify **X** and **Y**.

6. $^{27}_{13}\text{Al}$ can absorb an alpha particle with the emission of a neutron, forming a product **Y**.
    Write a nuclear equation to illustrate this reaction and identify **Y**.

Exercise 3.13   Half-life

1. For each of the following pairs, state whether or not both species have the same half-life.
    a) 1 g ^{212}Pb and 100 g ^{212}Pb
    b) 1 g ^{212}Pb and 1 g ^{212}Pb^{2+}
    c) 1 mol ^{210}Pb and 1 mol ^{212}Pb
    d) 1 mol ^{210}Pb and 1 mol ^{210}PbO

2. ^{24}Na is a radioactive isotope of sodium with a half-life of 15 hours. A sample of ^{24}Na has a mass of 200 g.
    a) What is meant by half-life?
    b) What will be the mass of the sample after 120 hours?

3. The initial radioactivity from a sample of actinium chloride is 120 counts/minute.
    If the half-life of actinium is 6 hours, how long will it take for the sample of the chloride to reach a reading of 15 counts/minute?

4. The rate of alpha emission from a 48 day old sample of a radioactive isotope was found to be a quarter of that of the original sample.
    What is the half-life of the sample?

5. After 15 days a sample contained 7.5×10^{21} atoms of radioactive bismuth, half-life 5 days.
    How many atoms were in the sample originally?

6. The isotope $^{131}_{53}$I is radioactive and is manufactured for medicinal use.
    If, 24 days after manufacture, only 32.75 g of an original one mole sample of radioactive iodine remains, calculate the half-life of the isotope $^{131}_{53}$I.

7. The radioactive isotope $^{210}_{84}$Po decays to $^{206}_{82}$Pb, which is stable.
    Calculate the mass of lead which would be formed from 1 mol of $^{210}_{84}$Po after two half-lives.

8. The half-life of a radioisotope is 2 min.
   a) Draw a graph to show the variation with time of the intensity of radiation due to the decay of a 10 g sample which has an intensity of 40 counts/minute.
   b) Using the same scale and axes add a dotted line to show what the graph would be for a 5 g sample.

9. A radioisotope **X** decays to give a stable product. The approximate decay curve is shown.

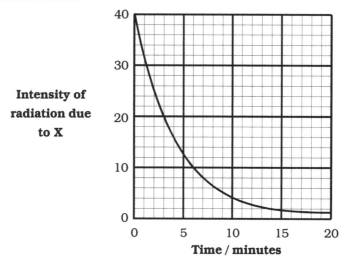

   a) What is the half-life of isotope **X**?
   b) Use your data booklet to find the half-life of ^{210}Tl.
   c) Copy the graph (no graph paper required), and add a dotted line to show the decay curve of ^{210}Tl, assuming that it starts at the same intensity of radiation as isotope **X**.

10. A radioisotope used in a hospital has a half-life of 1.5 hours. It has a count rate of 8000 counts min^{-1} at 9.00 a.m.
    a) What would the count rate be at 1.30 p.m. on the same day?
    b) An aqueous solution of a compound containing the radioisotope was prepared.
       What effect would this have on the half-life?

11. Samples of radium oxide and radium sulphate both contain the same radioisotope.

   Why does a 1 g sample of the oxide show a different intensity of radiation from the sulphate?

12. Polonium-218 is an alpha emitting radioisotope.

   After 6 min the mass of the radioisotope was found to be one eighth of the original.

   What is the half-life of the radioisotope?

13. $^{210}_{84}$Po, which has a half-life of 140 days, decays by α-emission to give a stable isotope.

   How many atoms of a 4.2 g sample of $^{210}_{84}$Po will remain unchanged after 280 days?

14. An 8 g sample of $^{24}_{11}$Na undergoes β-decay to form $^{24}_{12}$Mg as shown in the graph below.

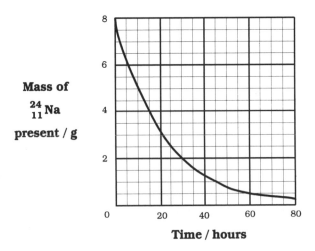

Mass of
$^{24}_{11}$**Na**
present / g

Time / hours

a) From the graph, what is the half-life of $^{24}_{11}$Na?

b) What mass of product would be formed from the sample after 45 hours?

15. The decay curve for the radioisotope tritium, $^{3}_{1}H$ is shown below.

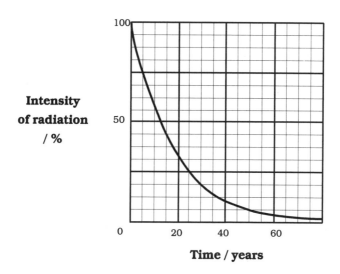

Intensity of radiation / %

Time / years

a) i) From the graph, what is the half-life of tritium?

ii) Calculate the time taken for the radioactivity to fall to 1/8th of its original value.

b) If the temperature of the tritium sample is increased, how would this affect its rate of decay?

17. The radio-isotope $^{131}_{53}I$ is used in hospitals. It has a half-life of 8 days and decays to give a stable product.

A bag of hospital linen contaminated with iodine $^{131}_{53}I$ was found to give a count rate of 320 counts s^{-1}.

a) Using graph paper, draw a graph to show how the count rate of the linen will change with time.

b) Hospitals are not allowed to dispose of material contaminated with $^{131}_{53}I$ until the count rate has fallen to 30 counts s^{-1}.

Use your graph to determine how long the bag of linen must be stored before disposal.

Prescribed Practical Activities

1. A student was given the following experiment.

> **Experiment**:
> To find the number of coulombs required to produce one mole of hydrogen by electrolysing dilute sulphuric acid.

   a) Draw a diagram of the nickel plating apparatus that could be used in the experiment.
   Label the diagram clearly.
   b) Which measurements would have to be made in the experiment?

2. In the laboratory preparation of an ester, sodium hydrogen carbonate is added at the end of the reaction.
   a) Why is this done?
   b) What evidence, apart from smell, shows that a new substance is formed?

3. The apparatus below was used by a student to find the enthalpies of combustion of alcohols.

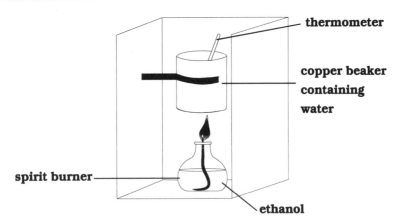

   a) List all the measurements the student should make to find the enthalpy of combustion of ethanol.
   b) What precaution was taken to minimise heat loss during the experiment?

4. The following table of results was obtained in the redox titration of vitamin C solution with iodine solution.

> | 1st titre | = | 25.60 cm^3 |
> | 2nd   .. | = | 25.20 cm^3 |
> | 3rd   .. | = | 25.30 cm^3 |

a) State the volume of iodine solution that should be used to calculate the concentration of the vitamin C solution.

b) How would the end-point of the reaction be identified?

5. The following results are taken from the notebook of a student who was trying to confirm Hess's Law.

> Experiment 1 - Addition of sodium hydroxide solid to hydrochloric acid
> $$NaOH(s) + HCl(aq) \rightarrow NaCl(aq) + H_2O(l)$$
> $\Delta T = 8.2\,°C$
>
> Experiment 2 - Addition of sodium hydroxide solution to hydrochloric acid
> $$NaOH(aq) + HCl(aq) \rightarrow NaCl(aq) + H_2O(l)$$
> Initial Temperature of HCl(aq) -T$_1$ = 21.7 °C
> Initial Temperature of NaOH(aq) -T$_2$ = 22.1 °C
> Highest temperature during experiment = 28.6 °C
> ΔT =
>
> Experiment 3 -

a) Calculate ΔT for experiment 2 .

b) Outline a third experiment which would have to be carried out in order to confirm Hess's Law.

6. Part of a workcard outlining the laboratory preparation of an ester is shown below.

PREPARATION OF AN ESTER.

1. Mix 1 cm^3 of the alcohol with 1 cm^3 of the alkanoic acid in a test tube.
2. Wrap a piece of paper soaked in cold water around the test tube and hold in place as shown in the diagram.
3.

4.

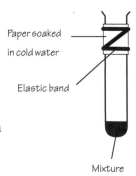

Paper soaked in cold water

Elastic band

5. After 20 minutes, pour the contents of the test tube into a beaker containing sodium hydrogen carbonate solution.

Mixture

Write down appropriate instructions for steps 3 and 4 to complete the workcard.

7. The decomposition of hydrogen peroxide can be used to investigate the effect of pH on enzyme activity.
   a) Name an enzyme which can be used in this investigation.
   b) Describe how the enzyme activity can be measured.

8. A technician was checking the concentration of a solution of vitamin C by titrating 25.0 cm^3 portions of the solution with iodine solution.

The technician's results are shown in the following table.

Titration	1	2	3
Titre volume / cm^3	16.5	15.8	15.8

a) Why would the technician ignore the result of the first titration when calculating the mean titre volume?

b) The picture shows a trainee technician taking a burette reading while carrying out a vitamin C / iodine titration.

Identify **four** points of bad practice in his technique.

9. A student tried to confirm Hess's Law using the reactions shown.

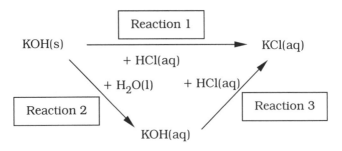

In reaction 1, the student measured the mass of KOH(s) and the temperature change of the reaction mixture.

a)   Which further measurement would have been taken?

b)   Describe a precaution which should be taken to minimise heat loss during the experiment.

10. Iodine solution was titrated with sodium thiosulphate solution, using starch indicator.

$$I_2(aq) \quad + \quad 2S_2O_3^{2-}(aq) \quad \rightarrow \quad 2I^-(aq) \quad + \quad S_4O_6^{2-}(aq)$$

The results of three titrations are shown in the table.

Experiment	Volume of thiosulphate / cm³
1	22.90
2	22.40
3	22.50

a)   What colour change would show that the titration was complete?

b)   Why was the volume of sodium thiosulphate to be used in the calculation taken to be 22.45 cm³ although this is **not** the average of the three titres in the table?

11. A student studied the effect of varying the concentration of iodide ions on the rate of reaction between hydrogen peroxide and an acidified solution of potassium iodide.

$$H_2O_2(aq) + 2H^+(aq) + 2I^-(aq) \rightarrow 2H_2O(l) + I_2(aq)$$

The course of this reaction was followed by carrying it out in the presence of small quantities of starch and sodium thiosulphate.

a) What is the purpose of the solution of thiosulphate ions?

b) Why is starch added?

12. Part of a workcard is shown.

WORKCARD

To find the effect of varying the concentration of iodide ions on the rate of reaction between hydrogen peroxide and an acidified solution of potassium iodide:

$$H_2O_2(aq) + 2H^+(aq) + 2I^-(aq) \rightarrow 2H_2O(l) + I_2(aq)$$

Procedure

1. Using syringes make up the following mixtures in five dry 100 cm³ glass beakers.

Mixture	1	2	3	4	5
Volume of sulphuric acid / cm³	10				
Volume of sodium thiosulphate / cm³	10				
Volume of starch / cm³	1				
Volume of potassium iodide / cm³	25	20	15	10	5
Volume of water / cm³	0				

a) Copy and complete the table in the first step of the procedure.

b) What is the colour change of the indicator which shows the end of the reaction?

13. Part of a workcard is shown.

WORKCARD

To find the effect of varying temperature on the rate of the reaction between oxalic acid and an acidified solution of potassium permanganate:

$$5(COOH)_2(aq) + 6H^+(aq) + 2MnO_4^-(aq) \rightarrow 2Mn^{2+}(aq) + 10CO_2(g) + 8H_2O(l)$$

Procedure
1. Using syringes, add 5 cm^3 of sulphuric acid, 2 cm^3 of potassium permanganate solution and 40 cm^3 of water to a 100 cm^3 clean, dry, glass beaker.
2. Heat the mixture to about 40 °C, measure and record the exact temperature.
3. Measure 1 cm^3 of oxalic acid solution into a syringe.
4. Start the timer and then add the oxalic acid to the mixture in the beaker.
5. When the reaction mixture just turns colourless, stop the timer and record the time (in seconds).
6. Repeat the experiment, but heat the initial sulphuric acid / potassium permanganate mixture to 50 °C.

State **four** ways of improving the investigation procedure.

14. Catalase is an enzyme which catalyses the decomposition of hydrogen peroxide:

$$2H_2O_2(aq) \quad \rightarrow \quad 2H_2O(l) \quad + \quad O_2(g)$$

a) Draw a labelled diagram of the apparatus that could be used to investigate the effect of temperature change on enzyme activity.

b) In this experiment, four approximate temperatures have to be accurately measured.
Explain the meaning of the terms **approximate** and **accurately**.

15. Esters are important and useful compounds. They occur in nature and can also be made in the laboratory.
a) Name the catalyst used in the laboratory preparation of an ester.
b) How can the ester be separated from the unreacted alcohol and acid?

16. Jean studied the effect of varying temperature on the rate of the reaction between oxalic acid and an acidified solution of potassium permanganate.

$$5(COOH)_2(aq) + 6H^+(aq) + 2MnO_4^-(aq) \rightarrow 2Mn^{2+}(aq) + 10CO_2(g) + 8H_2O(l)$$

In the first experiment she started by adding 5 cm^3 of sulphuric acid, 2 cm^3 of potassium permanganate solution and 40 cm^3 of water to a 100 cm^3 dry glass beaker.
She heated the mixture to about 40 °C and placed the beaker on a white tile. She then measured 1 cm^3 of oxalic acid solution, concentration 0.2 mol l^{-1}, with a syringe.

a) Copy and complete the sentence below to state how the course of the reaction could be followed.
   " Initially the reaction mixture is purple in colour due to the presence of _ _ _ _ ions, but it will turn _ _ _ _ as soon as they are used up."

b) What volume and concentration of oxalic acid solution would have been used in subsequent experiments?

c) Apart from volumes, what measurements would have been taken in each experiment?

17. Aldehydes can be oxidised by a mild oxidising agent.
   a) Name **three** mild oxidising agents.
   b) For each oxidising agent, describe the observation that shows an oxidation reaction is taking place.
   c) Why is a water bath used when heating aldehydes and ketones?
   d) Apart from wearing eye protection, state **one** precaution that should be taken when working with aldehydes and ketones.

18. Part of a workcard is shown.

WORKCARD

To find the number of coulombs required to produce one mole of hydrogen by electrolysing dilute sulphuric acid.

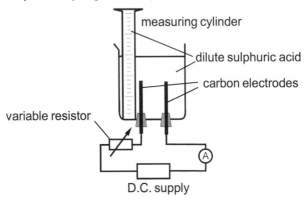

measuring cylinder

dilute sulphuric acid

carbon electrodes

variable resistor

D.C. supply

1. Assemble the apparatus as shown. **(Do not switch on.)**
2. Set the voltage to 6 V D.C.
3. Switch on and adjust the variable resistor to give a current of 0.5 A.
4. Switch off.

a) What is the next step before switching the current back on again?

b) In addition to the current, what measurements should be taken?

Problem Solving

1.   The first step in the industrial extraction of aluminium is to obtain
     aluminium oxide from the ore called bauxite.
     The ore is crushed. It is then digested, under pressure, with sodium
     hydroxide solution. The resulting mixture is filtered and the residue
     (containing large amounts of iron(III) oxide) is removed.
     The filtrate is seeded with a little aluminium oxide in order to produce
     large amounts of aluminium hydroxide. Sodium hydroxide solution is
     also formed.
     The aluminium hydroxide passes to a rotary kiln where it is roasted to
     form pure aluminium oxide.

     The flow chart summarises the production of aluminium oxide.

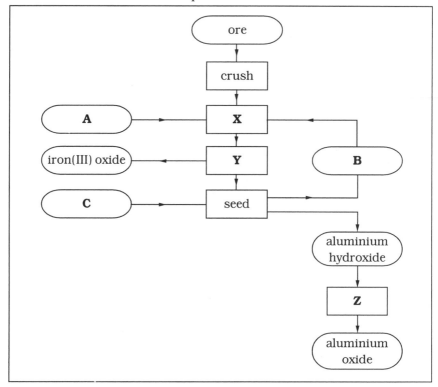

     a)   Name the chemicals **A**, **B** and **C**.
     b)   Name the processes **X**, **Y** and **Z**.

2. Sulphuric acid can be prepared in industry by the Chamber Process. The following chemical reactions are involved.

Sulphur is burned to produce sulphur dioxide.

Sulphur dioxide reacts with water to produce sulphurous acid.

Nitric oxide is produced by the catalytic oxidation of ammonia; water is also a product of this reaction.

Nitric oxide reacts with oxygen to form nitrogen dioxide.

Nitrogen dioxide reacts with sulphurous acid to form sulphuric acid and regenerate nitric oxide.

The flow diagram shows the production of sulphuric acid by the Chamber Process.

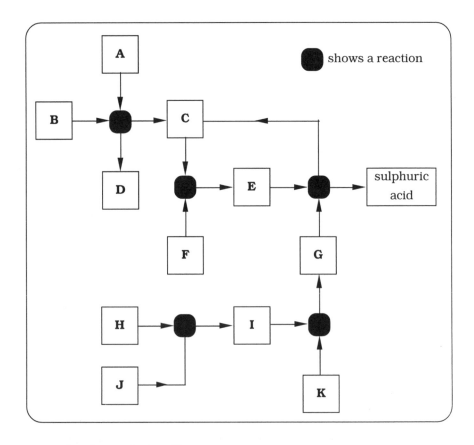

Name the chemicals **A** to **K**.

3. Acetone, widely used as a solvent, is manufactured from cumene. Cumene is oxidised by air to form cumene hydroperoxide. The cleavage of this compound produces a mixture of acetone and phenol which is separated by distillation.

Draw a flow chart to summarise the manufacture of acetone from cumene.

In your flow chart use ⬭ to represent chemicals

and ▭ to represent processes.

4. Prefixes can be used to indicate the number of atoms in a molecule.

Term	Number of atoms per molecule	Example
diatomic	2	hydrogen chloride
triatomic	3	carbon dioxide
tetra-atomic	4	sulphur trioxide
penta-atomic	5	tetrachloromethane
hexa-atomic	6	phosphorus pentachloride

a) What term is used to describe the molecule shown?

b) Name a hexa-atomic molecule, containing carbon, which will decolourise bromine water.

c) Write a formula for a carbon compound consisting of penta-atomic molecules with a molecular mass of 85.

5. The structural formulae for some acids containing oxygen are shown.

Acid	Strength	Structure
nitric	strong	$O{=}{>}N{-}OH$ (with two O double bonded to N)
nitrous	weak	$O{=}N{-}OH$
sulphuric	strong	(O double bonds to S, with two OH groups)
sulphurous	weak	$O{=}S$ with two OH groups

a) What strucural feature appears to determine the strength of these acids?

b) Chloric acid, $HClO_3$, is a strong acid.
Draw its full structural formula.

6. The compound diazomethane, CH_2N_2, undergoes an unusual reaction called **insertion**. Under certain experimental conditions, the CH_2 group produced can insert itself into **any** bond which includes an atom of hydrogen.

eg

$$H{-}\underset{\underset{H}{|}}{\overset{\overset{H}{|}}{C}}{-}OH \xrightarrow{CH_2N_2}$$

product 1:
$$H{-}\underset{\underset{H}{|}}{\overset{\overset{H}{|}}{C}}{-}\underset{\underset{H}{|}}{\overset{\overset{H}{|}}{C}}{-}OH$$

product 2:
$$H{-}\underset{\underset{H}{|}}{\overset{\overset{H}{|}}{C}}{-}O{-}\underset{\underset{H}{|}}{\overset{\overset{H}{|}}{C}}{-}H$$

Nitrogen is a product in every reaction.

Draw the full structural formula for the **three** organic products formed when diazomethane reacts with ethanol.

7. The idea of **oxidation number** leads to a systematic method of naming inorganic compounds.

The systematic name of $KClO_3$ is potassium chlorate(V) where the Roman numeral in brackets represents the oxidation number of the chlorine atom.

Simplified rules for working out the oxidation numbers are:

all Group 1 metals have an oxidation number of 1+;

oxygen has an oxidation number of -2;

the sum of the oxidation numbers of all atoms in the formula of a compound is zero.

Give the information corresponding to **A**, **B**, **C**, **D** and **E** which would complete the table below.

Formula	Oxidation number of non-oxygen atom in the negative ion	Systematic name	Charge on the negative ion
$KClO_3$	+5	potassium chlorate(V)	-1
Na_2SO_4	+6	**A**	-2
B	+7	potassium iodate(VII)	-1
Na_3PO_4	**C**	**D**	**E**

8. Markovnikoff's Rule

Addition of hydrogen chloride to an alkene can give two products. Markovnikoff observed that the hydrogen of the hydrogen chloride mainly attaches to the carbon atom of the double bond which already has the most hydrogens **directly** attached to it.

a) Draw the full structural formula for the major product formed when hydrogen chloride reacts with propene.

b) Why is it **not** necessary to consider Markovnikoff's rule when hydrogen chloride reacts with but-2-ene?

9. Complex ions are formed when molecules or ions join to a central metal ion by means of co-ordinate bonds.

The molecules or ions joining the central metal ion are called ligands and the total number of bonds being made to the central ion is known as the co-ordination number.

The charge of the complex ion is the combined charges of the central ion and the ligands.

a) Give the information corresponding to **P**, **Q**, **R** and **S** which would complete the table below.

Central metal ion	Ligand	Co-ordination number	Structure of complex ion	Charge of complex ion
Al^{3+}	F^-	**P**	(structure) F — Al with six F ligands	3-
Q	NH_3	4	(structure) Cu with four NH_3 ligands	2+
Fe^{2+}	CN^-	6	(structure) Fe with six CN ligands	**R**
Co^{2+}	**S**	6	(structure) Co with three ethylenediamine ligands	2+

b) A coloured complex ion is formed when solutions of nickel(II) sulphate react with solutions of ammonia.

The colour is most intense when the concentration of complex ions is greatest.

The graph shows the colour intensity when different volumes of equimolar nickel(II) sulphate and ammonia react.

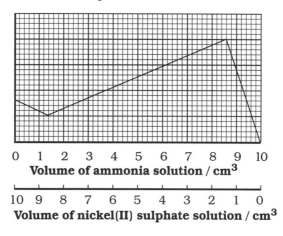

i) Describe how a student could have carried out this experiment.

ii) What ratio of ammonia to nickel(II) sulphate gives the highest colour intensity?

10.

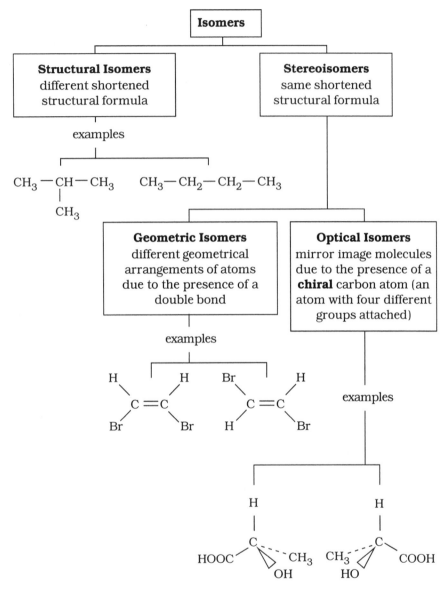

Isomers

Structural Isomers
different shortened
structural formula

Stereoisomers
same shortened
structural formula

examples

$CH_3 - CH - CH_3$
     |
    CH_3

$CH_3 - CH_2 - CH_2 - CH_3$

Geometric Isomers
different geometrical
arrangements of atoms
due to the presence of a
double bond

Optical Isomers
mirror image molecules
due to the presence of a
chiral carbon atom (an
atom with four different
groups attached)

examples

examples

a) Draw a structural isomer of 1,2-dibromoethane.

b) Draw the geometric isomers of but-2-ene.

c) Copy and complete the diagram to show the
lightest alkane molecule containing a **chiral**
carbon atom.

11. In a mass spectrometer, the energy of an electron beam can break bonds in molecules to form fragments containing groups of atoms. The positions of the peaks (or lines) in a mass spectrum correspond to the masses of the fragments which are formed.

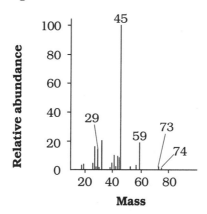

In the mass spectrum shown, the peaks at masses 29, 45, and 59 are formed by the breaking of carbon to carbon bonds in:

$$\begin{array}{ccccccc} & H & & H & & H & & H \\ & | & & | & & | & & | \\ H- & C & - & C & - & C & - & C & -H \\ & | & & | & & | & & | \\ & H & & H & & OH & & H \end{array}$$

a) Give the information corresponding to **F** and **G** in the table below.

Relative mass	Formula of fragment
29	C_2H_5
45	**F**
59	**G**

b) Suggest what causes the peaks at masses just below the main peak at 45, eg at 44, 43, 42 and 41.

12. X-ray diffraction is a technique used to determine the structure of molecules. It is the electrons in the atoms of the molecule which diffract the X-rays. From the diffraction pattern, an electron-density contour map of the molecule can be constructed.

The following map was obtained using an aromatic compound with molecular formula $C_6H_3Cl_3O$.

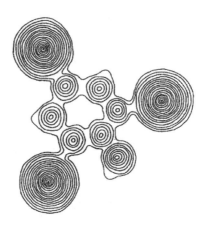

a) Suggest why the hydrogen atoms do not show up clearly in the electron-density contour map.

b) Draw the full strucural formula for this compound.

c) Draw the electron-density contour map that would be obtained for methanoic acid:

$$H-C \overset{\displaystyle O}{\underset{\displaystyle O-H}{}}$$

13. The bonds in organic molecules absorb infra-red radiation. The same bond in different molecules always absorbs infra-red radiation of similar wavenumber. For example, the C–H bond absorbs in the range 2800-3000 wavenumbers (cm^{-1}).

The following diagrams refer to three different organic liquids.

Pentane   CH₃CH₂CH₂CH₂CH₃

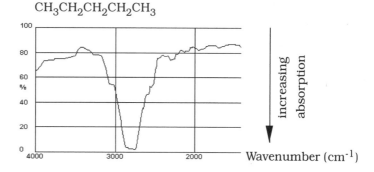

Pentan-2-one   CH₃CH₂CH₂COCH₃

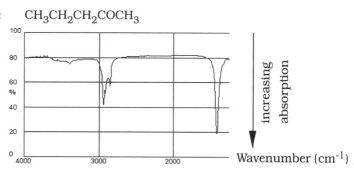

Pentan-1-ol   CH₃CH₂CH₂CH₂CH₂OH

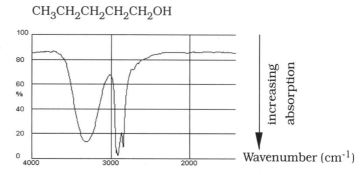

a)   The absorption at 1710 cm⁻¹ in the spectrum of pentan-2-one is absent from the spectrum of pentane and pentan-1-ol. Which bond could be responsible for this absorption?

b)   Sketch a graph to show the absorptions you would predict for pentanoic acid.

14. Differential thermal analysis (DTA) is a technique used to investigate changes which occur in substances when they are heated. This technique involves measuring the temperature difference between a test substance and a reference substance when both are heated.

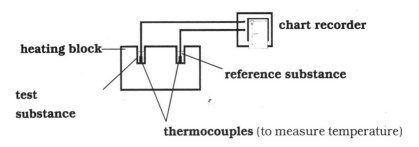

chart recorder

heating block

reference substance

test substance

thermocouples (to measure temperature)

As soon as a change occurs in the test substance, its temperature (T_T) will differ from that of the reference substance (T_R).

The following DTA curve was obtained when using calcium oxalate (CaC_2O_4) as the test substance.

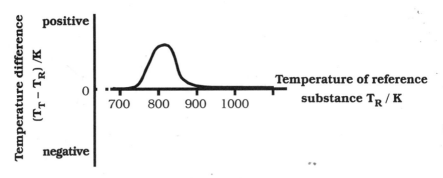

The peak corresponds to the change: $CaC_2O_4 \rightarrow CaCO_3 + CO$

This change occurs at 725 K

a) Why can it be concluded that the rise in the DTA curve is due to the change being exothermic?

b) Suggest a property which a substance must have to make it suitable as a reference substance in DTA analysis.

c) Selenium melts at 490 K.

Draw the DTA curve which would be expected if selenium was heated in the DTA apparatus in the range 440 K to 700 K.